STOP ACTING LIKE A SELLER AND START THINKING LIKE A BUYER

STOP ACTING LIKE A SELLER AND START THINKING LIKE A BUYER

IMPROVE SALES EFFECTIVENESS BY HELPING CUSTOMERS BUY

Jerry Acuff
with **Wally Wood**

BICENTENNIAL
1807
WILEY
2007
BICENTENNIAL

John Wiley & Sons, Inc.

Published by John Wiley & Sons, Inc., Hoboken, New Jersey.
Published simultaneously in Canada.

Wiley Bicentennial Logo: Richard J. Pacifico

For general information on our other products and services or for technical support,
please contact our Customer Care Department within the United States at (800) 762-
2974, outside the United States at (317) 572-3993 or fax (317) 572-4002.

Wiley also publishes its books in a variety of electronic formats. Some content that
appears in print may not be available in electronic books. For more information about
Wiley products, visit our web site at www.wiley.com.

Library of Congress Cataloging-in-Publication Data:

Acuff, Jerry, 1949-
   Stop acting like a seller and start thinking like a buyer : improve sales
effectiveness by helping customers buy / Jerry Acuff with Wally Wood.
      p.   cm.
   ISBN: 978-0-470-06834-2 (cloth)
   1. Selling.   2. Customer relations.   I. Wood, Wally.   II. Title.
HF5438.25.A28   2007
658.85—dc22

                                                          2006036783

Printed in the United States of America.

10   9   8   7

CONTENTS

CONTENTS

ACKNOWLEDGMENTS

Writing a book, like most things in life, is best accomplished by getting help and learning from others. This book would never have come about if it weren't for the help of so many. I will try to recognize as many as I can here although I am certain I will inadvertently leave someone out.

First, I must thank Laurie Harting at John Wiley & Sons. She is such a professional and a joy to work with. Her belief in this book and her constant guidance made this book possible.

My coauthor, Wally Wood, who has become my close friend now after three (well two and a half) books, deserves a standing ovation for his contribution. He makes me think, he knows how to write, and he constantly challenged both of us to make this the best book we could write. Wally's wife Marian also played an important role with this book as she has with each book we have written, and I am so grateful to her for her help. Mary Maki did yeoman service transcribing our taped interviews.

My family has always given me total support and allowed me the time to devote to this effort when I am certain they would have had me doing something else. My wife, Maryann, and my son, Ryan Joseph, deserve special recognition because of the sacrifices they made so that I could complete this book. I owe them so much and feel grateful and humbled by their love and support. I am also thankful to the rest of my family, my daughter Laura, my father Gerald Acuff Sr., and my brothers and sisters (Jan, Jude, Joanne, and Tracey) for their undying support and constant inspiration.

So many people gave generously of their time to share the ideas and stories that truly enrich this book and make the concepts advanced here come to life. To each of them, I say thank you, thank you, thank you—Mike Accardi, Melvin Boaz, Lesley Boyer, Mike Bradley, Sean Feeney, Greg Genova, Shari Kulkis, Jack Martin, Linda Mullen, Henry Potts, Valerie Sokolosky, Tim Wackel, Dan Weilbaker, and Anthony Yim.

I also owe a huge debt of gratitude to the employees of DELTA POINT, the firm my partner Mike MacLeod and I are fortunate enough to lead. Mike is a mile-a-minute thinker whose ideas make our firm better, and so many of those ideas are embedded in this book. He is an incredible sounding board and his ability to think broadly, strategically, and practically is what makes him such an invaluable resource to me personally and to our firm. To Maryann Ryan, Nancy MacLeod, Michael Michel, Michelle Gammon, and Dan McNamara, I must also give thanks. Your devotion to our firm's excellence has not only helped us be successful, but also generates new ideas about sales excellence on a daily basis. Lori Champion deserves mention because she has edited so much of what we have written. She has a way of taking what Wally and I think is good and making it even better. Thank you, Lori.

Last and most importantly, I want to thank all of our clients who are truly focused on the knowledge, messaging, and relationships of their sales organizations and are committed to sales and communication excellence and have thought well enough of us to partner with us at DELTA POINT. Without them, many of these ideas would never have seen the light of day.

Some of these clients deserve special mention—in particular, David Snow and Jesus Leal (who have been with me since day one), and Tim Walbert, who brought us to his company, Abbott, in the early days of DELTA POINT. Their friendship and support is unequaled.

I would also like to recognize one leadership team that we have worked closely with—Eric Von Borcke, Dwayne Wright, and Edward Scheidler. They have been incredibly supportive and they are special leaders.

Others who have made powerful contributions to our learning and need special recognition include Anne Cobuzzi, Louis Day, Don Dwyer, Adam Foster, Dave Ilconich, Theresa Martinez, Dan Orlando, Dave Tang, Beth Tench, Mike Tilbury (who to the best of our recollection was the first to give us the phrase "think like a buyer"), Mike Weber, Ron Wickline, and Rod Wooten.

We would be remiss if we didn't mention other clients who have been so important to our learning: Paul Alexander, Stan Austin, Ronan Barrett, Mike Bell, Drew Bernhardt, Michael Betel, Jack Britts, Jen Campagna, Elaine Campbell, Dave Capriotti, Charlie Carr, Ciro Carvaggio, Patrick Citchdon, Jim Elliott, Joe Elliott, Steve Engelhardt, Tammi Gaskins, Heidi Gautier, Heidi Gearhart, Cathy Geddes, Georges Gemayel, Kevin Hamill, George Hampton, Scott Hicks, Pat Higgins,

ACKNOWLEDGMENTS

Doug Houden, Jeff Hyman, Scott Iteen, Marianne Jackson, Huw Jones, Larry Kich, Tom Klein, Zahir Ladhani, Denise Levasseur, Debi Limones, Fred Lord, Matt Mays, Rob Mc-Cune, Jeannie McGuire, Connie McLaughlin-Miley, Deanne Melloy, Molly Moyle, Jayne Patterson, Al Paulson, Chris Posner, Chuck Peipher, Nick Recchioni, Carol Richards, Nick Sarandis, Maire Simington, Big Jim Smith, Todd N. Smith, Cathy Strizzi, Alex Thole, Erika Togneri, Debbie Wilson, and Roy Williams.

Each person mentioned here understands that there is quite a difference between selling someone something and helping someone buy something. Thanks to every person who contributed to our learning and the development of our thinking about buying versus selling.

SECTION I

START WITH THE RIGHT MIND-SET

CHAPTER 1

IF PEOPLE LOVE TO BUY, WE SHOULD HELP THEM BUY

The United States economy is about $10 trillion, due in no small part to the fact that people love to buy. But as much as people love to buy, they also do not like to be "sold." Few more profound things have ever been said or written on the subject than what sales guru Jeffrey Gitomer says in his *Little Red Book of Selling*.[1] "People hate to be sold but they love to buy." When you buy a car, a television set, a computer, you don't say to associates, friends, or your mother-in-law, "Look what the salesman sold me!" You say, "Look what I bought." As a people, we Americans like to make purchases. We like going to the mall, getting a new car, buying a new house, or looking for a new TV. It feels really good when we buy something we want.

Yet while most people love to buy, buying from a salesperson is all too often an adversarial situation, and rarely is it much fun. Far too many salespeople *act* like sellers rather than *think* like buyers. The customer wants one thing; the salesperson wants another. The customer wants a particular car, but the salesperson would rather sell the model the dealer is pushing this month. The customer wants an inexpensive 28-inch color TV, but the salesperson wants to sell a 45-inch flat-panel set because it carries a higher commission. That attitude is not helping customers buy and is not customer-focused—no wonder most of us hate being sold.

Although some salespeople may realize a certain degree of sales success, most never achieve sales greatness because they don't sell in a way that makes the buying experience positive. Unless you marry mind-set and relationship building with a good sales process, you're unlikely to ever reach greatness in selling, and that's what this book is about—how to reach sales greatness.

The formula for sales greatness is simple: The right mind-set + A proven sales process + A commitment to building valuable business relationships = Sales greatness.

The negative attitude toward salespeople is as true in business-to-business sales as in consumer sales. Surveys find executives in industry regularly frustrated because salespeople often have difficulty communicating effectively; they lack adequate knowledge of the customer's company and business; they come across as too aggressive; and often they overpromise and under-deliver. It's no surprise that most businesspeople—including salespeople—have a negative view of selling. The facts speak for themselves.

Consider Valerie Sokolosky's recent experience. Valerie, the president of the Dallas, Texas, leadership development firm Valerie & Company, was in Santa Fe, New Mexico, on vacation with her husband. Eight years ago they bought two pieces of art from an artist who now has his own gallery in Santa Fe. Their first stop on the vacation was the artist's new gallery where they introduced themselves to the young saleswoman. "We told her we had two nice pieces of the artist's work. We'd stopped by to say hello to the artist and see his latest work. We were in the gallery for an hour, and all the woman could do was try to sell us more art. 'Well, what about this? What about that?' She never once asked, 'Where will it go? What is your style?' She just tried to push his new style: 'Isn't this wonderful? This would look lovely in your home.' She didn't know what kind of a home we had. As we walked out the door, she handed me their card with her e-mail address and said, 'Please send me a picture of your condominium so I can pick out art for you.'" She didn't listen and she certainly wasn't thinking like a buyer. She was acting like a seller.

I could fill a book with such stories since everyone has one. If you play a word-association game with "sales" or "salesperson," the words people most often associate are: "obnoxious," "aggressive," "manipulative," "insincere," and the like. We tend to think of salespeople in terms of telemarketers at dinnertime, car salespeople, and pushy insurance reps. Based on many bad experiences, most of us believe salespeople are interested mainly in themselves and will do almost anything to make a sale. That you are reading this book suggests that you do not fit this stereotype . . . and if you embrace the book's message, it is likely that buyers will not tar you with the stereotype once they deal with you.

Because most people hate to be sold (for good reason), generations of smart sales executives have thought about ways to overcome this aversion. They've developed all kinds of techniques to wear down prospective customers' resistance and to manipulate those prospects into doing what the salesperson knows . . . or believes . . . or hopes will be best for them. "Buy my product; it'll be good for you. Trust me."

FOCUS ON THE BUYING, NOT THE SELLING

This book will not add to the mountain of advice on how to overcome customer aversion and maneuver prospects into committing to your product or service. Instead of offering yet another selling model, this book offers a buying model. My goal is to help sales representatives and managers understand and learn how to use a dramatically more effective sales process from beginning to end.

Much of what has been taught historically about the transaction we call a *sale* has focused on the sales side. Most traditional sales models—Integrity Selling, SPIN Selling, Strategic Selling, and the like—have focused on how you sell *to* people, what should happen to get them to commit to your company's product or service, to convince them, to influence them, to persuade them—rather than show you how to walk through this process together.

Most of the traditional sales processes teach you how to make a sale. Nevertheless, processes alone will not gain you the credibility you need for prospective customers to see you as someone who brings value. If our goal is to sell more, we must be valued more and considered as credible, so that when we advance ideas, buyers really listen to us. The only way to achieve this is to have the right mind-set, incorporate an effective process, and understand the critical role of building relationships (Figure 1.1).

In this book, I focus on how you can make it easier for customers to buy. The distinction is that rather than something you are doing *to them,* this is something they want to do *for themselves* (although they may not know it at the beginning of the exchange). The only way they will want to do it for themselves is if they believe whatever you are promoting is a fit and is in their best interest.

In a perfect world, the most significant role, by far, that the salesperson plays is opening customers' minds rather than closing them. Traditional sales techniques tend to show reps how to break into an already closed mind, which is hard, discouraging

Figure 1.1

A Buying Model Requires

Mind-Set

Sales Process

Relationships

---

work. The chances for success are higher when you consistently open customers' minds by the way you deal with them, thus enabling them to listen to you differently.

TOWARD A DEFINITION OF SELLING

To think like a buyer, it is first necessary to properly define selling both individually and organizationally. Ask a hundred salespeople in a single company, "What is selling?" and the chances are you'll hear a hundred definitions: "Selling is solving problems" or "Selling is meeting people's needs" or (among the more academically inclined) "Selling involves the use of persuasive communication to negotiate mutually beneficial agreements."

This lack of consistency is a problem because what we think is crucial to the way we act. When an organization does not have a single definition of selling, its salespeople behave differently by their own definitions—not good for the salespeople and certainly not good for the company.

Worse, salespeople sometimes think they must do things on behalf of their companies that conflict with how they see themselves

9

as human beings. They believe that to sell they must be pushy, and most of us don't want to be pushy. They believe they must apply pressure or perhaps be manipulative in some way, but most of us don't want to high-pressure or to manipulate people. Most of us would rather opt out. Interestingly, to succeed in sales, you don't have to be someone you don't want to be, but you do need to have passion, commitment, and curiosity. And it is far easier to be passionate, have commitment, and be curious when you are working with the right definition of selling and those beliefs drive your behaviors.

So we need a definition of selling that asks salespeople to do things that are consistent with the person they see themselves as being and still accomplishes the business goal. Years ago, I listened to a Nightingale-Conant tape series by Fred Herman, and his definition of selling has guided me now for over 20 years. Herman said that selling involves two intimately connected concepts: (1) *Selling is teaching,* and (2) *selling is finding out what people want and helping them get it.*

First, selling is teaching. In every successful sale, some education takes place; the prospect, and often the salesperson, learns something each party did not know before. Although most prospects and customers don't want to think that salespeople educate, ideally learning is one of the things that will happen. When it does, it just may trigger behavior change.

Teaching is not lecturing, mechanically delivering a core marketing message for your brand, or rattling off features and benefits. Think about the best teachers you had in school. I suspect they did not talk at you all the time. Great teachers are masters at involving their students, engendering interaction, and making them think. That is what great salespeople do—inform, involve, engage, and provoke thought. They connect with people, generate meaningful dialogue, and stimulate customers to open their minds in much the way an exceptional teacher connects with students.

Second, selling is indeed finding out what people want and helping them get it—much easier to say than to do. Remember that people buy what they want, not necessarily what they need (although the two may overlap). Do people know what they truly want? Most people have not clearly or comprehensively thought through their situation, or they may not even know exactly what is happening or available as a solution. They may think they want one thing when another product or service may actually meet their needs better.

One of my friends went into a new Apple store to replace a Macintosh computer. He had done some research and decided the new Power Mac G5 was the model he wanted. Before demonstrating any computer, however, the Apple salesperson asked several key questions: What do you use your computer for? Do you do a lot of graphics or work with several large files at one time? Several more questions established my friend's real need—and the Power Mac G5 wasn't it. The salesperson recommended an iMac G5. It would do everything my friend wanted to do (and considerably more), and the package was $400 less than the Power Mac.

Because this salesperson thought like a buyer, she was able to help the prospect buy what he truly wanted and needed—not what he thought he needed. Simple, yet powerful.

So, what is selling? We accept Fred Herman's definition: "Selling is teaching, and selling is finding out what people want and helping them get it." We don't sell; we help customers buy.

On an everyday basis, you are simply trying to see (step by step, side by side with your prospects) if and how your product or service (or both) is a fit for what they want. When salespeople genuinely believe this selling definition, it fundamentally changes how they approach customers. No longer do they say to themselves (or, by their behavior, to prospects), "I'm here to sell today" or "I have to make a sale today." No longer should they have to say, "The number of calls today really matters." They are now in the business of learning whether their prospects want or need what their company offers. And that's it. Where that fit exists, salespeople won't have to sell because customers will buy, and that is a far more powerful force than any slick sales technique.

The Holy Grail of selling is credibility, a function of expertise plus trustworthiness. Expertise reflects your knowledge, not just of your product but of your complete offering, your competitors, your customers and their needs, your customer's marketplace, and more. You develop trustworthiness by relationship building and by what you say.

If prospective customers see you as credible, they are more likely to act on your suggestions and advice. They listen to you differently than if they see you as just another salesperson out to make a sale. They believe that you personally bring value to them. The only way to create this environment of trust and credibility is by thinking like a buyer rather than acting like a seller.

The very best salespeople do this by teaching and by helping people to discover what they really want. When they define selling and approach customers in this way, buying is most likely to occur. It isn't easy, that's for sure. But it works and it is honorable.

START WITH THE RIGHT MIND-SET

One of the elements missing from most sales training or selling approaches is the central role that the salesperson's mind-set plays. Your beliefs drive your behavior. If you believe you are shy, you act like a shy person. If you believe you are outgoing, you will talk to anyone. If you believe you can never get a fair break, events and other people will conspire to hold you back. If you believe you can accomplish almost anything, you will. What you believe the selling process to be is incredibly important to how you sell—and most salespeople have not thought it through.

A sales representative must have the right mind-set to be truly customer-focused. You can't care about the sale. You can't focus exclusively on your company's goals. Unless you balance building the business relationship with representing your company's product or service, you won't achieve long-term sales success. It is not simply that salespeople don't think like buyers. They don't have a correct view of selling and are not focused on the relationship as a key part of the sales experience.

The salesperson's job is to help prospects understand their alternatives and then have a planned conversation with them about the product and how it fits into their current need, or unrecognized want, or both. Interestingly, once the customer recognizes a want and its ramifications, it is often one your product answers. For you, it becomes the "Aha!" moment that salespeople seek. Not only do you make the sale, but now you are trusted and valued, and the customer desires a professional relationship with you. (In Chapter 6, I discuss in detail how you can learn what people really want.)

You must have the right mind-set, a good process, and understand the critical role of building relationships—this book is designed to help you reach that understanding.

THE FIVE RULES OF BUYING

There are, I am convinced, five basic rules of buying:

Rule 1: You will sell significantly more *if you think like a buyer than if you act like a seller.* (I believe this so strongly, I paraphrased the rule for the book's title.)

Rule 2: The quality of your business is directly linked to the desire of your prospective customer to want to have a conversation with you.

Rule 3: The size of your business is directly linked to your ability to ask a customer questions that *engender thinking.*

Rule 4: High-pressure environments tend to create little exchange, which results in a lack of meaningful dialogue.

Rule 5: Low-pressure environments tend to create greater exchange and customer receptivity. (No-pressure environments create nothing; avoid them. There must be some pressure to move the customer forward.)

The paradox is that the less you care about the sale, the more you sell. When you genuinely care about the buyer, then you

14

think like the buyer. You begin to understand what things are important to the buyer. You are curious to uncover how this buyer thinks and makes decisions—what is important to that person.

Remember that virtually everybody wants to find ways to achieve more, to be secure, to have a sense of belonging, to have excitement in life, to have more fun and enjoyment, to feel self-confident, to have more prestige, to be more influential—or all of the above. Most of the products and services that conscientious salespeople sell are solutions that bring someone an emotional or psychological reward. (I recognize that unscrupulous salespeople exist who peddle shoddy or harmful goods. They care only about themselves and routinely give the profession a bad name.)

The customers who want those things you're selling that help them achieve more, have more fun, be more effective, and the rest—want them only when you can actively engage them in the process. When they participate and you build a positive relationship, it is easier to identify their needs, even their unstated and secret needs. Without a valued business relationship, however, it is very unlikely you will get beyond the stated need.

WHY TRADITIONAL TECHNIQUES LIVE ON

Thinking like a buyer seems so logical and works so well, it raises the question of why so many sales managers continue to train their sales staff in the traditional techniques of approaching prospects, negotiating sales resistance, overcoming objections, and closing deals.

I suspect there are several reasons. Managers are doing what they were taught by their managers . . . they have an illusion of knowledge . . . the techniques *do* work some of the time . . . and the law of large numbers applies here.

Most sales managers come out of the sales department. As salespeople, they were successful—that's how they got promoted—and they were relatively successful having been taught by an earlier generation of sales managers. If doing what they did got them this far, why change? *Because the world has changed.* But most salespeople are not students of sales, they don't educate themselves about human behavior; it is easier for them to accept what someone says than to learn on their own.

They often have an illusion of knowledge from having studied books such as *Getting to YES* by Roger Fisher, William L. Ury, and Bruce Patton,[2] which teaches how to negotiate agreements without giving in; and *Getting Past No* by William L. Ury which teaches how to negotiate your way from confrontation to cooperation.[3] (Thinking like a buyer changes the dynamics of any negotiation dramatically, by the way.)

The illusion of knowledge is simply a belief that this traditional sales technique works—and I know why. The illusion of knowledge is far more powerful than ignorance, because ignorance can usually be demonstrated and corrected with education. The illusion of knowledge is difficult to change because people believe that what they think is correct, when in fact it is wrong (or insufficient).

Finally, the law of large numbers can help traditional selling techniques. If you call on enough people, you will get some results. When you call on enough prospects, you will run into some who need your product or service. They will purchase despite you, not because of you. Even the most inept salesperson makes some sales.

Selling processes tend to fall into one of three buckets. There are the traditional selling models: "Let me teach you how to sell anybody anything." There are the persuasive models: "Let me teach you how to ask gimmicky trick questions that will get people to sign on the dotted line." And there are the customer-focused selling models: "Sell people only the things they want or need."

For several reasons, many people have been successful using traditional sales tactics. One is that they use these techniques in combination with a genuine belief in the product's value. What comes through to the customer is a passion for the product that often compensates for mediocre sales tactics. A salesperson who really has that passion will transfer it to a certain number of prospective customers. Not all buyers have the constitution to tell a salesperson they are not going to buy. Some sales representatives will make a clever enough argument that prospects will be sort of talked into the sale. Some people can go into a car dealership and unless they have the right constitution, the salesperson can talk them into buying a car. Probably at a higher price than they should have paid. Because our society recognizes this state of affairs, we have laws saying that you can return almost anything you buy within 72 hours.

Traditional selling techniques work to some degree, but the process I describe in this book works far more effectively for far more salespeople in far more industries. The question is not, will you have success, but what kind of success will you have? Any time you can involve the buyer in the process, you increase the likelihood you will be successful in making a sale, and you will increase the frequency with which you sell.

WHEN NOT TO SELL

This strategy lets you proactively help more people buy than would have otherwise, because they actively participate in the process. They talk to you because they believe you are interested in them and their problems (and you are). They are genuinely interested in learning more from you because they believe it makes sense for them to listen (and it does). People like to buy. The problem is they don't want to buy from someone who acts like every other salesperson.

Fred Herman also said, *"If people want what we don't have, we have no right to sell them what we do have."* Most salespeople find this statement enormously liberating because they are no longer in a position to pressure people to buy something that does not truly fit their wants or needs. Your goal is to find out what prospects and customers want and help them get it. If your organization cannot help them, you should not spend any more of your invaluable time trying to change the conditions. You should openly state that your offering is not a good fit and when you do, you lay the foundation for a future opportunity almost every time. Consider my experience in a BMW showroom.

I wanted a bigger car, and I was trying to decide between a BMW 7 Series, which is around $80,000 and an Infiniti Q45, which is around $60,000. I am a loyal Infiniti customer, but I wanted to look at the BMW. Nobody pounced on me in the showroom, so I was able to sit in the cars. I was enjoying that experience when the salesman came over and asked, "How do you like the car?"

I said, "Actually, I like it a lot."

"Are you in the market for a car now?"

"I've been thinking about getting another car, so I'll probably buy in the next two or three months."

"What other cars are you considering?"

"I'm looking at the Q45."

He said, "That's a great car."

"Yes, I like it. I've driven several Infiniti models. I really like this car, but I'm having a hard time understanding the difference in the price. What makes this car worth $20,000 more than the Infiniti?"

Here's what the salesman said: "How much do you like driving? Really driving the car, as opposed to just a car as a mode of transportation."

"Well . . . I really prefer a car as a mode of transportation. The driving experience, frankly, is lost on me."

"Then this isn't worth the money to you, Mr. Acuff. You should get the Infiniti. The Infiniti is a great car. It's got almost all the bells and whistles this has. The BMW is about driving a car. If you don't really love driving a car, I wouldn't spend the money if I were you."

What did this do for the salesman's credibility? He openly told me this product wasn't a good fit for me. By doing so, he laid the foundation for a future sale because I cannot think about another car without going over and giving the BMW a shot. What does this say about the way BMW does business? I don't know. But I have told this story a hundred times, and if even one person has looked at a BMW because of it, it was good for BMW.

Once you realize your product or service is not a good fit for the buyer, you've got to openly say so. There's incredible power in telling someone you're not good for them if you truly are not—at least not now. It builds your credibility, and you have no idea what that will do for you over the long term. Sometimes nothing, but if you plant enough seeds, some of them will sprout.

Think about it. As soon as people suspect they are being sold, most of them think, okay, I recognize what this is. It's a sales call, and I'm going to respond the way I've learned to respond as a buyer or a prospect. Either I'm going to feign interest and get this person away from me as quickly as I can, or I'm going to act as if I acquiesce when I really and truly don't, because I don't ever have to call them back.

But if you signal that this is an interaction where the prospective customer's wants and needs are what matter most, people are far more likely to stay involved in exchange—at least until they see whether there is something that would benefit them.

Another approach is to think the way buyers think and approach buyers with language and strategy that are consistent with how people like to buy. People like to buy from people who are credible, who are friendly, honest, and don't bash the competition. They like to buy from people who don't sound as if they know everything. They like to buy from people who understand that their product—though it may be very good—isn't the greatest thing since microwave popcorn. They like to buy from people who make them feel they are trustworthy. They like to buy from people who are real.

Success is always a by-product of doing the right thing. It is also about exhibiting professional beliefs or behaviors. Some say that the key difference between an amateur and a professional is preparation and practice—it seems to make sense. So, if you are positive and confident about your definition of selling, then you are most likely doing the right thing for your customers and success will follow.

The important point here is that you obtain credibility by not focusing on yourself. Don't think, "How do I make this sale?" "How do I make my quota?" or "How do I get to yes?" Think like a buyer, don't act like a seller.

CHAPTER 2

EIGHT LAWS OF SALES INTENT

Let me boldly state that in selling intent is everything. By *intent,* I mean purpose. Your intent is your state of mind at the time of an action—having your mind focused on a specific objective. The related idea of *intention* is your plan to do something, or the course of action you plan to follow. The critical concept to internalize and think deeply about is this: *If* intent is your state of mind at the time you carry out an action, then what is *your* intent when you are interacting with a customer or prospect? The plain and simple answer to that question has a far-reaching impact on your sales success.

So when thinking about intent, ask yourself two things: What is my purpose? And, what do I plan to do? Solana Beach consultant and author Brian Tracy says, "The first thing you should feed your mind is purpose. Customers respond to the energy and enthusiasm that are created by a sense of purpose."[1]

Simplistically, if my intent or purpose is to sell you, I am *me-focused.* If my intent is to teach you, or to find out what you want and help you get it, I am *other-focused.* When you sell based on a definition of selling that is other-focused, your action is to understand the situation before you prescribe or recommend. You are more likely to carefully prepare your interactions with customers and make sure you know and ask questions about them, their business, the competitor, and the competitor's business before you start suggesting why and how your product or service might be a fit.

The right intent opens minds, the wrong intent closes minds. If you approach a situation with the wrong intent, it will likely be immediately transparent. People are so accustomed to salespeople being "me-focused" or pushing a sale that their radar is always up. They are poised to ignore or run at the first sign of a hard sell. On the other hand, if you approach a situation with pure intent, it may not be as easy to convey in short order. For customers to sense and feel the right intent, they must listen, ask questions and evaluate your approach to them and their situation. They are more apt to engage in a conversation with you and have meaningful dialogue when they feel that your intent is pure.

To be a great salesperson, I believe we should learn and act on the *Eight Laws of Sales Intent* every single day:

1. I intend to have empathy, to see things from the customer's point of view.

2. I intend to focus on them and not on me.

3. I intend to find people who truly want what I am offering.

4. I intend to be seen as different, unique, and the consummate professional.

5. I intend to *master* the knowledge I need to be seen as an expert in my business.

6. I intend to prepare for every call, not because it is important to me but because it is important to my customers and prospects.

7. I intend to use words and find language that will resonate with my prospects and will be compelling.

8. I intend to have an internal focus of control because I understand I am responsible for the outcomes of my actions.

Let's consider the implications of each of these laws.

I INTEND TO HAVE EMPATHY

I am passionate about *being other-focused*. I first began to understand this when I was a district sales manager in Birmingham, Alabama. I learned quickly that success means having the ability to identify with and understand another person's feelings or difficulties. Salespeople who have empathy try to put themselves in the customer's moccasins. They want to understand the customer's problems, challenges, and stresses, if possible from the inside. Research on interpersonal relationships indicates that empathy is one of the most important requirements for building positive, constructive relationships, both personal and business.

This is an idea whose time is coming. Recently, *BusinessWeek* reported on the change at Altera Corporation, a San Jose, California, chipmaker. In the late 1990s, salesman Mike Dionne juggled 25 accounts, but when the bubble burst in 2000, "Dionne's sales dried up fast, and no amount of wheedling could persuade many of his customers to meet with him. He talked a lot but listened for the wrong things. The market had changed, but Dionne hadn't."

Altera's CEO, John P. Daane, has now spent $11 million on empathy training to help the sales force and salespeople like Dionne identify with customers' situations, feelings, and motives. "We're trying to understand and develop better customer relationships," he says. "We're still in the very early innings of using customer empathy to get there." About 10 percent of the sales representatives found the training so foreign that they quit rather than continue. "People don't really want to see life exactly as the customer sees it. They just want to sell stuff," said an Altera consultant. So don't think living this law will be so easy.

Mike Dionne, from Altera, has gotten with the program. Looking at the world from the customer's point of view has changed the way he does business. He now has only seven accounts and takes much longer to close a deal, mostly because he listens much more. Recently Dionne met with an executive at a Massachusetts-based medical firm for the first time. He reiterated what he had said to the prospect on the phone: Altera was looking at how it should invest in the medical field. "For 90 minutes Dionne sat quietly as the potential customer described the technology he planned to buy and the obstacles he expected," the magazine reported. "Dionne never said Altera wanted to sell him chips. 'You could tell he was jazzed,' says Dionne. 'He was comfortable, leaning back in his chair and talking freely.'" Even if Dionne does not close a sale with this prospect, CEO Daane says he is happy with the approach, believing—based on Altera's strong financial results—that seeing things from the customer's point of view will ultimately pay off.[2]

One way to see the world from the customer's perspective is to spend time with them observing how their operation works. When I was in Birmingham, I required each of my sales representatives to work in a customer's office at least a half-day each quarter. We would ask customers (usually ones we didn't know so well) if we could spend a half-day as volunteers working in their office. We would tell them it was a requirement for our sales representatives' learning and development (which it was) and that we would be happy to do whatever the customer asked us to do. Our entire objective was to see what life is like on the other side of the desk. Our salespeople answered the phone, they did filing, they cleaned out closets, and in one office the rep spent a half-day installing toilet paper holders.

The results were amazing. My salespeople began to quickly see that the 10 to 15 minutes they spent in that office was just a snapshot in time, and while it might have been the most important part of their day, to the customer it was far less important. They learned that everyone has a difficult job and that everybody is important. The other thing that happened in almost every case is that we improved our relationship with that office. In exchange for letting us work in their world, we would buy the office lunch. From these experiences, what our people learned about their customers and their point of view was invaluable. We did this for the entire time I was the district manager, and I am convinced that it played an important role in making us one of the top districts in the country every year for eight consecutive years.

Shari Kulkis, HCV division sales manager for Roche Laboratories, is naturally empathetic. She talks to the entire office staff, not just the physician she's calling on because she's learned that everybody is important. She observes the magazines in the office, the pictures on the walls. When she is invited into doctors' private offices, she sees what they covet and what they collect. "It is usually displayed on their shelf," she says. "Then, you just ask questions. Well, what does the doctor like to do on the weekends?" This mind-set has to enabled her not only to sell her company's products but to learn about her customers. The more she knows about them, their concerns and challenges, and the more they know she cares about their problems, the easier it is for them to buy from her. Her intent is not to have a relationship just with the decision maker, but with everybody. This has enabled her to learn helpful facts in her offices that most other salespeople never learn. That can only happen when you always try to see the world from the perspective of others.

I INTEND TO FOCUS ON THEM NOT ME

Great salespeople are crystal clear about their intent. Before they pick up a phone or walk into an office their intention is always to do what is in the best interest of the customer. They focus on customers and not on themselves and their products.

Salespeople (or their marketing departments) often tend to predetermine that prospects may be good candidates for their products; even cold calls are not random. Too often when we assume that prospects need what we are selling, we do not effectively probe for real problems or concerns. We just offer up what we've got without ever trying to learn if there is a fit. The end result is that salespeople hold far more presentations than true sales conversations, and this is the farthest thing from focusing on prospects.

There is a relevant analogy here between the actions of salespeople and physicians. Competent physicians never presume to know a patient's condition without a full workup and understanding of the patient's symptoms and vital signs. Only after doctors have a clear idea of the disease (because they have listened to the patient) do they select the proper therapeutic approach. Too often, salespeople skip diagnosing and go directly to the action step, in essence a prescriptive action designed to achieve a desired result.

If you *tell* customers without trying to understand their situation, it's the throw-it-against-the-wall-and-see-if-it-sticks sales process. Sometimes salespeople are so caught up in their own wants and needs that they are almost oblivious to the customer's. My friend Anthony Yim, a telecom sales professional, describes not understanding a prospect's situation at all.

One day, Anthony's boss told him to call on a Japanese bank in New York City, a new prospect. Anthony had no relationship with the company or its people, had never called on them before. His company had heard that the bank's contract for telecommunication services might be coming up for renewal. "I was calling on them because we heard they were going to pick somebody for a contract. It was pure sales revenue acquisition mentality," Anthony tells me. His intent was to sell something, not to learn the bank's situation or needs.

At the bank, Anthony met with two executives who were extremely hostile. "At their best, they were just acknowledging I was in the room. At their worst, they were grilling me left and right. 'What can you do? Why would we even think about you?' They were so unpleasant—and I didn't like it."

While Anthony would always welcome another account, he was growing busy with other, less demanding, prospects. He told himself he did not really need to be calling on these guys and take their abuse. The bank already had a large contract with one competitor and a small contract with another competitor, and they seemed to be happy with both. So Anthony asked himself, what am I doing here letting them jerk me around? But the bank's contract was in fact expiring; and apparently going through the motions, the bankers he met with followed up with a three-page proposal request. At his end, Anthony also went through the motions, returning a proposal. He says, "At no time did the thought cross my mind to try to build the relationship.

To try to find out what was going on—to try to learn something personal about these guys—to try to do something different. My attitude was: I'll just carry my boss's orders and try to sell something. See what happens. Throw stuff against the wall and hope something sticks."

Anthony had a second meeting after submitting the proposal and it was more uncomfortable than the first. "When I came back to my office, I was barely under control. I wanted to kick things, but instead, I told four or five people and how awful this situation was. Later that afternoon, I got a message from the bank—'We have these new requirements.' I looked at the fax and there were six or seven things they wanted that we couldn't do. Having been upset about the whole situation, I decided to blow them off. Just ignore them. Not a professional thing to do, but I thought it was warranted. Just let them go. I'd given them a proposal. If they send me a purchase order I'll write it up, but that's it . . . having done nothing to engage these people in any meaningful dialogue."

The bank, not unexpectedly, did not send a purchase order, and Anthony put the experience out of his mind.

About four months later, one of Anthony's colleagues was stopped by one of the two bank executives at a trade show. Spotting the colleague's badge, the banker asked, "What happened to you guys? We were told to give you the business. But your guy never came back."

In retrospect, Anthony realizes he did not initially approach the bank with pure intent. He was looking, first, to sell something and, once in the meeting, to defend himself from the perceived hostility of the customers. He was focused on himself.

"I should have done something to defuse the hostility, reduce it so we could have had a little more of a discussion. I couldn't

32

have a dialogue because they were very combative. But, I think now they were just being combative because they were protecting themselves. At the time, I felt I was being played for better pricing and they'd just go back to their existing vendors. It would have helped if they'd told me what was really going on."

If Anthony's intent had been focused on his client, he would have attempted to diagnose the bank's problem before prescribing his company's solution. The bank executives might still have been abrasive, but if Anthony could have convinced them he was more interested in helping them solve their problem than in getting an order, it might have reduced the friction. And he would have had a signed order.

I INTEND TO FIND PEOPLE WHO TRULY WANT WHAT I AM OFFERING

This seems blindingly obvious. Why waste your time (or theirs) on people who don't want what you sell? Organizations and salespeople work hard to identify the most likely prospective customers of their product or service. New software and online services now help small companies find sales leads. Online social networking services like LinkedIn, Jigsaw, Spoke, and iProfile can help you identify contacts through mutual acquaintances.

While these tools can be useful, the problem remains: You don't know if people truly want what you're selling until you talk to them (and neither do they). They may not in fact want what you are selling, although from the outside they seem to be likely prospects. They may want what you're selling, but not strongly enough to make a decision now or to take the time to listen to your proposal. They may want it, but it's the end of the budget period or the CEO has just instituted a cost-cutting program or their credit cards are maxed out. They may also want it and need it and not realize it. (That is why you are there!) Prospects have a gazillion reasons for not acting now. It took Linda Mullen six years to engage one likely prospect.

Linda is president of Altus, Inc. and an agency owner and wardrobe consultant for Doncaster, a line of women's clothing sold direct. Wardrobe consultants across the United States sell the Doncaster line. The company ships the clothing—coats, jackets, skirts, pants, sweaters, accessories, and more—to the consultants' homes. The consultants then schedule appointments for clients to see the clothes. Linda holds six two-week trunk shows in her home, which is in the Philadelphia area; and she is now holding shows in San Francisco, San Diego, and Washington, DC.

"Ninety-nine percent of the women I work with are professional women," says Linda. "Mostly attorneys, firm partners, and women who own their own businesses, or are very high up the corporate ladder. It took me six years to get one woman— the head of the litigation department for a major law firm—in for a trunk show. A colleague had referred her, and I called her regularly for six years. I sent her literature and letters, followed up, but nothing happened. Finally, she came to a trunk show one Wednesday night. It was obvious she's a Type A personality, very pressed for time. We went around the room and in 45 minutes, she created a $6,000 order. I couldn't write it fast enough. I gave her a glass of wine while I wrote up the order so she could get right out. After the close, I do a fitting. So I went to her home and did the fitting, which took maybe a half hour or so. She tried everything on, I pinned it, took the clothes to the tailor, and delivered them back to her. She could not believe the service and loved it. She came in for the second part of the season and I wrote the order without her because she had no time to wait. We met for 35 minutes and she spent $800 a minute. To say she is an enthusiastic shopper is an understatement. I adore her and she appreciates me. I think she's sent me more referrals than any other customer, something she continues to do today." Linda's intention to find people who truly want what she offers (personalized service, time savings, fashion ideas from someone with fashion expertise, etc.) enables her to develop strong relationships with her prospects and clients because they know she is not looking for a sale. She is looking for a fit, which they appreciate, and they are glad to refer her to other people they know.

I INTEND TO BE SEEN AS THE CONSUMMATE PROFESSIONAL

How do your clients perceive you? Are you among the masses of ordinary salespeople or are you truly different? In a perfect world, customers see great salespeople as unique resources, so the question is: "In the minds of your customers, how different—and valuable—do you want to be versus your competition?"

It is easy to be like everybody else—just do what everybody else does. Your intent will be clear and you will sell to the relatively small percentage of likely prospects who can be persuaded easily.

If you want to be seen as different, then you have to *be* different. You have to believe that the less you care about the sale, the more you sell. Your intent is long-term focused not short-term focused. It is (usually) not to make an immediate sale, but to create a winning relationship or partnership with this company, prospect, or client because you know that over time loyal customers are like an annuity. Your objective is not a sales call but a sales conversation, and ultimately, the sale if you deserve it. Only after you listen and learn something about what your prospects are trying to accomplish (or think they are trying to accomplish), should the sales process turn to your hypothesis or to the premise you think might make sense for this situation.

Consider Jack Martin. When Jack graduated from college in 1969, he wanted to become a financial planner. He went through rigorous training where his company taught him how to telephone people and sell them stock. The last week of his training, Jack had a major revelation. He thought, "This makes no sense. I am twenty-three years old and they are asking me to call people, rich people who I don't know, and ask them to give me their money. That seems stupid to me." He told his boss he wasn't going to do it.

His boss asked, "Well, what are you going to do?" And Jack answered, "I am going to call on people in person."

"Jack, it will never work. You won't get in the door."

Jack said, "I don't care; I'm going to try because it has to work better than calling strangers on the phone."

Jack headed to downtown Chicago and started knocking on doors. For two weeks nobody would talk to him. Finally, he tried the CEO of one of the eight largest accounting firms in the country. Jack told the receptionist, "I'm here to see the CEO." She asked if he had an appointment, and he admitted he did not. She asked, "What is this about?" and Jack said, "It's a personal matter."

Jack tells me that within five minutes he was sitting in the CEO's office where he introduced himself and identified the securities company he was working for. Then he said, "It occurred to me that people like you wouldn't want to invest with stock brokers or financial planners unless you actually met them. So I thought I would just come by and introduce myself and find out a little bit about you. Do you mind telling me something about yourself?"

Jack says the guy talked for an hour and practically told him his whole life story. At the end of the hour the guy looked at his watch and said, "Holy smokes, Jack, I have to go. Give me your card; I'll call you."

Two weeks later, the CEO called Jack and placed an order for $5 million in bonds. I asked Jack what the commission was on $5 million in bonds. In 1969, it was $95,000—not bad for a 23-year-old. Jack Martin retired at age 49 in no small part on business he received from that one firm, since many other senior executives became clients.

Why did these executives invest with Jack? They made their purchases because Jack *was different*. The product he was selling was similar to products other young financial planners were selling. Jack's story is a great example of the point that when customers perceive products as similar, the people selling them must be perceived as different.

I INTEND TO MASTER THE KNOWLEDGE TO BE SEEN AS AN EXPERT IN MY BUSINESS

I talk about knowledge in detail in Chapter 3, so for now I will say only that salespeople who take the time to master the knowledge necessary to be an expert in their field are seen as truly exceptional. Therefore, whether customers fully agree with any given point, they still view such salespeople as consultative, credible, and trustworthy. When you master your entire job's essential knowledge, you are most capable in front of prospects and customers because this deep knowledge builds the confidence needed to be great at selling.

Many companies (and salespeople) define *knowledge* only as information about their own products and applications or services, but in reality it includes so much more. In addition to basic product and service knowledge, you also need comprehensive command of:

- Your competition or competing premise/hypothesis
- Your prospects/customers and their issues and challenges
- Yourself and how your communication style and personality are likely to affect other people

I am not talking about simply having good information. Good information is the cost of entry. You must know more than your product's features and benefits. You should know how they apply in all situations and to the prospect's needs. You should also know the issues and challenges the customer faces. This kind of knowledge allows you to think of your offering on a big-picture scale. When you learn to think "big picture" versus "narrow situation," you can communicate with your clients on many aspects and levels of their business instead of just your product (being other focused), and you will be seen as a valued problem solver and consultant.

I INTEND TO PREPARE FOR EVERY CALL

This Law of Sales Intent is particularly important because it not only stands alone but is an inherent part of all the Laws of Sales Intent. As mentioned at the beginning of this chapter, you have to prepare for every sales interaction with the right purpose or objective.

Now it is time to ask yourself, "Why am I calling on this customer?" It is not for small talk. It is not to make a new friend. It is a planned conversation to sell more to customers or prospects who really want what you have because it is important to them. If your products represent a reasonable, even valuable benefit for the prospect or the prospect's customers, then you should be proud and passionate in what you say. That alone, however, won't consummate "buying" on behalf of your prospect.

Begin your preparation for this interaction by silently stating your purpose. Say to yourself, "I am going in there to diagnose, not prescribe. I am going in there to have a conversation. I'm not going in there to make a sale (although that may happen). I am going in there to find out what this customer wants and to engender thinking."

Make notes and write down the questions that will help you find out the information you need to determine if there is a fit.

Full preparation is a requirement for success. This is not so easy to do at first, but when done well and habitually, the results are incredible.

The value premise you are advancing is an important aspect. If you prepare a reasonable value premise, you can probably find a place for your product with many more potential customers by simply and routinely changing your intent. These ideas do not work if you have a lousy product or service because there will be a profound disconnect between who you are, what you say, and the product you sell. You must have a product or service with a logical value proposition or some true uniqueness in the marketplace. If it does, you can find people who need or want it—if you focus on them and not on you.

When you prepare better, you will find that you make fewer sales calls, and you will facilitate more conversations that are far more likely to lead to sales success.

I INTEND TO FIND LANGUAGE THAT WILL RESONATE

Your ability to facilitate the conversation, advance your ideas, or sell a product or service is directly related to how well you stimulate thinking in the other person. To do so, you want to use words and language that resonate with your prospects and customers and do not repel them. Words matter! Your ability to create a low pressure and safe environment with words and language that mix the right amount of logic and emotion is crucial to your sales success.

Sometimes salespeople have a series of great presentations and great meetings and leave wondering why their message didn't resonate. They believe the logic is impeccable. They believe that the customer—based on everything they know, everything they have read, everything they have researched on the Web or annual report, and everything they have learned from other people—is an ideal client. Why wouldn't they want to save money? Why wouldn't they want a more reliable system? Why wouldn't they want better technology? These salespeople make presentations that advance a hypothesis and logic that make perfect sense to them—and the prospect doesn't buy.

Remember, prospects often come with a negative bias toward salespeople. One reason they don't buy is because the salesperson's language does not resonate. The words the salesperson uses say that this is an effort to sell them something they don't need . . . or don't need right now . . . or don't need enough to buy at the price.

In your preparation, think about using words and stories that get your clients to think differently about you and your product. So, plan the delivery of your value proposition and questions. Your intent is to use your words to gain new understanding for both of you. Sometimes during your conversation, you may have the opportunity to stimulate thinking about a situation in a different light.

One time when I was selling pharmaceuticals, a doctor told me, "I put five people on your drug . . . and four of them died." Not the start of a good sales call.

I said, "Let me ask you this: When you were sitting at the nurse's station and you were trying to decide what drug to put these people on, how many of these five people did you think would die?"

"I thought they would all die."

"Then, I don't think it sounds like such a bad drug."

I didn't try to defend the product at first. I didn't tell him why he was wrong, which almost certainly would have ended the conversation. By my question, I made him think. I took him back to a place in time where he was thinking about my product and then I let him connect the dots for himself. I helped him visualize making those decisions and recalling his thought process at those moments, which made all the difference. As the doctor revisited his reference point, he concluded for himself that my drug was a lifesaver, not a problem drug.

What if he had said, "I didn't think any of them would die"? Again, I would not have defended the product. In fact, that response would have suggested a question about the medication, and I would have tried to help the doctor get our product off the market.

This happens in the pharmaceutical industry. The FDA approves drugs and then physicians learn that they've got a problem. Had this been a drug like that, my personal value system would have forced me at the very least to investigate further to see if there really was a problem or if this doctor's experience was an anomaly. If the drug needed to be taken off the market, I would have pushed to have it removed.

By selecting my words carefully and making certain that my intention was to gain understanding of that specific situation, I could understand the doctor's position on my drug and stimulate his thinking on its success rate, not its failure rate. Customers need us to find words that resonate and bring our ideas to life. If we do not bring our ideas to life with words that resonate, the customer may never be able to verify our hypothesis, no matter how solid it is.

I INTEND TO HAVE AN INTERNAL LOCUS OF CONTROL

> People are always blaming their circumstances for what they are. I don't believe in circumstances. The people who get on in this world are the people who get up and look for the circumstances they want, and if they can't find them, make them.
>
> —George Bernard Shaw[3]

People with an internal locus of control see themselves as responsible for what happens as a result of their actions; they tend to believe that they, not the fates or company politics or other people, control their destiny. People with an external locus of control, on the other hand, see their environment or situation as more important in what happens to them than what they do or don't do. They tend to see luck more than effort as determining whether they succeed or fail, and they are more likely to view themselves as the victim in any given situation.

Research by Gerrard Macintosh concluded that "people with higher self esteem, an internal locus of control and greater empathy would be more likely to have a more relational time perspective, and therefore, be more likely to set goals and engage in behaviors that will foster long-term relationships."

By "relational time perspective" Macintosh means that some salespeople set short-term goals (that influence behavior), while others set long-term goals. People who have a longer time perspective see near-term goals as "building blocks" for longer-term goals. This is significant because salespeople with a short-term orientation tend to be more aggressive in persuasion and negotiation and are more inclined to try to close a sale on the first call. Salespeople with a longer time perspective tend to consider the past and future, says Macintosh, "and use a more cooperative integrative/problem-solving approach to selling." And the good news is that research has found a more relational selling behavior increases relationship quality and customer commitment to the firm.[4]

When you approach your business from an internal locus of control, you know that success is dependent on one thing—*you!* You realize that your intent is everything and that your intent drives your actions. You prepare differently and you introduce discussions differently. You *create* many more viable opportunities when you have a discussion with somebody who has an open mind because *you choose* the words to get them to listen to you differently.

Your actions in turn communicate your intent loud and clear. Take a look at a great example.

McNeil Consumer Products (Johnson & Johnson) took action years ago when seven people died mysteriously after taking Extra-Strength Tylenol. They immediately took 31 million bottles of Tylenol—all Tylenol, not just Extra-Strength—off pharmacy and supermarket shelves. Nobody has ever forgotten the way the corporation behaved consistent with their values, which is nothing more than pure intent. Intent drove Johnson & Johnson to do the right thing and intent is crucial for each of us to do the right thing in selling especially in the mind of the buyer. But there is one more component to mind-set that must be discussed.

The last component to having a mind-set designed for sales greatness is believing that to be great in front of the customer takes a commitment to excelling at messaging, having mastery of the knowledge necessary to be seen as an expert, and building your business with valuable business relationships. So let's now talk about the importance of knowledge, messaging, and relationships.

CHAPTER 3

BUILD YOUR KNOWLEDGE, MESSAGING, AND RELATIONSHIPS

What differentiates great salespeople from the merely good ones when they are in front of customers? The great ones start with the right mind-set—the pure intent I've been talking about—but what they say and do in front of their prospects ultimately determines whether they are effective or not.

Sales representative effectiveness in face-to-face situations is a function of salespeople believing that they must master three areas: knowledge, messaging, and relationships (KMR). If you believe that, then you will put forth the requisite effort to become proficient in all three. If you believe that KMR is important, your mind-set forces a decision—what am I going to do about this?

It is important to recognize immediately that *just* knowledge or *just* messaging or *just* relationships that makes the difference. Sales success requires the combination of all three skills and as well as a mental commitment to all three. Knowledge, messaging, and relationships are not just three critical concepts; they also involve your mind-set. In this chapter, I focus on both the mind-set and the concepts because they are impossible to separate.

In Chapter 2, I discussed the Laws of Sales Intent. This approach to mind-set infiltrates everything we do, especially the way we respond to Laws 5, 6, and 7. Mastering knowledge, preparing every call, and using words that will resonate play a significant role in the success of KMR, because without the right mind-set, you will not behave differently enough to have a profound effect.

Most companies focus on one or two of these elements as if they were stand-alone issues, but the truth is knowledge, messaging, and relationships are inextricably interwoven. As Figure 3.1 illustrates, any one impacts the other two. People with whom you have a great relationship are more likely to receive your message positively than if you have no relationship. You are also more likely to obtain more information from them because, through your good relationship, they trust you. If you have great knowledge, you are more likely to express your message well. If you express your message well, people are more likely to have a great relationship with you and give you more information.

Because all three elements are intertwined, the more successful you are with one element, the more likely it is you will be successful with the other two. To be thoroughly effective, you need to be aware of and develop all three.

Figure 3.1

THE KNOWLEDGE MIND-SET: WHAT YOU KNOW

Many salespeople have not mastered the knowledge required to be exceptional or to be seen by their prospects and customers as trusted advisors. I suspect this is because they do not truly understand or believe how important it is to master the knowledge needed for sales greatness. This is one side of the equation: having enough knowledge for your prospects and customers to value your suggestions and advice. You can't message what you don't know.

The other side of the equation is what the knowledge does for you. When you master all your job's essential knowledge, you are most capable in front of prospects and customers, and this level of knowledge builds your confidence and self-esteem.

Many companies define knowledge as product knowledge or technical knowledge and spend the bulk of their training budget to teach product (or service) features and benefits. Knowledge is significantly more robust than that. In addition to what we have talked about earlier it also includes understanding yourself and how your communication style and personality are likely to interact with another person. Moreover, knowledge is not simply about data but about mastery. As I have said, it is not enough simply to have accurate information; that is the price of entry. You must master the necessary information to be successful. You want to know and understand the larger context in which the customer functions. While you will be more successful if you can demonstrate that you understand the client's bigger picture, most salespeople lack this knowledge.

In contrast, my friend Mike Accardi, who sells packaging materials and systems for Wurzburg Inc. in Memphis, Tennessee, has spent 30 years developing his knowledge. Mike points out that if you truly partner with a customer, you don't have to sell; your customers will buy. "If after becoming a partner, you perform, you become a resource. You are no longer a vendor; you are a resource. You are part of the team."

As an example, Mike says that his largest customer, which ships thousands of packages a week, went through a period of constant flux. "The building was always being torn up and conveyers rerouted. They went through a major change three years ago. They brought in a consulting firm to help with the reorganization and introduced me, and from that day forward I met with the consulting firm almost every day. They called me with questions about everything—things you wouldn't think you would talk to a packaging person about, they would call me with. I was a consultant to the consultant, and would either handle it or immediately find somebody for them who would handle it. That's what I mean by being a resource."

Let me give you another example to show how knowledge is power: At one time, I sold a diabetes medication as an Alabama district manager for a pharmaceutical company. We had a competitor with an identical compound, and our customers said they made the decision on which to use based on price. We said our drug was less expensive, the competitor said their drug was less expensive, and we were both right. Depending on how a customer purchased, we could both claim we were less expensive.

I told my reps I wanted them to canvass every retail pharmacy in the state of Alabama and ask this question: "When a patient pays for a thirty-day supply of this drug, which is less expensive to the patient? Don't ask them what they cost. You don't have a right to know what the pharmacies charge their customers. But you do have a right to know if there's a difference in the cost."

I said I wanted them to record every store they called on because I wanted to know exactly where we had a cost advantage and where we didn't. I also wanted to know the cost differential among those stores that would provide that information, realizing that some would tell us and some wouldn't.

We learned that in 70 percent of the drugstores in Alabama, if a patient paid cash, their 30-day supply of our drug was less expensive than a 30-day supply of the other drug. That was the fact. So when I went to see a doctor, I would ask, "How important is the cost of these medications to your patients since the products are identical?" As you might expect, the doctor would say, "It is everything."

Then I would ask, "What cost are you most concerned about? The cost to the pharmacy?" (Which was the claim both companies had been making.) "Or are you concerned about the cost to the patient?" One hundred percent of the time, the doctors said, "I don't care what the pharmacy pays; my concern is what the patient pays."

I then said to the doctor, "Here's what I ask you to do. Have someone in your office call ten drug stores that your patients are likely to visit and ask the pharmacist, 'Which of these drugs is less expensive to the patient for a thirty-day supply?' Once you have the answer to that question from ten pharmacists, you will have done your own little market research and you will know the answer. At that point, you don't have to listen to me tell you we're less expensive, and you don't have to listen to them. But here is what I know because we have done our research: Our drug is less expensive to the patients in seven out of ten drug-stores in the state of Alabama. If you will have someone call ten pharmacies to find out for yourself, I'll buy that person lunch. If we are not less expensive than the other drug in seven out of ten cases, I'll buy lunch for everybody in your office."

At the end of the year, we were the only district among 70 in our company that outsold the competitor. Our competitor had twice as many salespeople in Alabama, but we had the only district in the United States with a larger market share than they had. We did it because we knew what was important to the customer. We could go into doctors' offices with confidence because we knew that in seven out of ten drugstores we were less expensive for the patients. We also knew that cost was the customers' major differentiator and concern. We were perfectly willing to have a doctor call ten drug stores, and if we weren't less expensive for whatever reason, we were willing to lose that business.

There is another lesson in this story. There are no parity products. Even products that are identical in chemical composition—or features . . . or benefits . . . or price . . . or convenience . . . or service—have something unique that will appeal to some customers. Ideally, a product will have several unique elements, and ideally the marketing department will have identified them and promoted them with great marketing messages to your prospective customers. But because this is not a perfect world, however, you may have to uncover those unique elements yourself and promote them to your prospects in your market. I'll talk about how in Chapter 7, I explain how to weave these elements into a compelling story.

Salespeople must understand the big picture as well as the issues and challenges that customers face within their businesses, and to do so, they need to get customers to talk about their challenges. To have the mind-set to be exceptional, you must seek this level of knowledge. It is relevant when you are selling almost anything. Most customers are pleased when you demonstrate an interest in their business; they want you to have some understanding of their larger issues; they want to believe that you know more and are interested in more than your narrow product or service.

Several Laws of Intent stress the importance of preparation in framing the questions you ask and the environment you create. Knowledge is imperative in your ability to prepare well. Those questions should encourage prospects and customers to talk about their broader business issues. Your ability to craft insightful questions will depend in large part on your knowledge because the more you know about a situation, the more perceptive your questions can be. Your knowledge enables you to focus your energies on the prospect, to listen more effectively, and to respond with greater empathy. You'll be in control of yourself and your side of the successful sales interaction because you will not be afraid of being asked questions for which you don't have an answer, let alone a good answer. Then you have to take all the information and use it in a sales conversation when it is appropriate.

Knowledge comes from many places—from training, from what you learn on the job, what you learn from other people, and what you learn on your own. You also gain knowledge through personal passion and curiosity. It is your mind-set—and only your mind-set—about knowledge that will drive you to seek out and learn the information necessary to become great, no matter what the sacrifice might be.

That sacrifice, or as some say, "burning the midnight oil," is a key element to your success. To master knowledge and become a resource to your customers, you must be willing to pay the price, which may be as painless as watching less television or as demanding as a graduate-level college course.

Mastery of knowledge serves as the catalyst to great messaging and valuable business relationships. Make up your mind to develop your expertise.

THE MESSAGING MIND-SET: HOW YOU EXPRESS IT

The second element in sales effectiveness in front of the customer is messaging—what you say and how you say what you say. As Mark Twain once noted, "The difference between the almost right word and the right word is really a large matter—it's the difference between the lightning bug and the lightning."

Your ability to articulate your message effectively is also a function of how much you know and your relationship with the customer. Ideally, what you say forces prospects and customers to think about topics in ways they had not thought before. Messaging is about creating effective communication that encourages buyers to want to know more because they sense, by your words and actions, that you can help them achieve some result that is important to them. They want to understand your perspective rather than just endure a sales call and count the seconds until you stop talking.

Messaging is not necessarily a carefully crafted sales message that you memorize and deliver or a script that you repeat for every prospect. Effective messaging involves a mind-set that looks at the big picture before you ever speak with the client. It is about preparing your message so that it engenders thinking and dialogue, while creating an atmosphere where the client is at ease and does not feel a lot of pressure. It includes some or all of these elements: questions, prefaces to questions, observations, requests, statements of fact, and, occasionally, opinion. (The BMW salesman who told me, in effect, that I should stick with Infiniti was expressing his opinion.)

This kind of preparation allows you to build a customized message for each prospect or client with whom you engage. Many companies make the mistake of sending reps out with a standardized script that they repeat to everyone; this is a dangerous approach because it can come off as a pitch. Dan Weilbaker, the McKesson Professor of Sales at Northern Illinois University, tells me that he and other faculty members talk to their sales students about standardized scripts: "They're not really good because you don't tailor them to the individual customer. On the other hand, I say that we all have a lot of little tape recorders in our heads and they are like sound bites, little prerecorded messages that always come out differently. If it's a topic you know well and you say something cogent, sometimes it's like, oh, where did that come from? It came from practice because you practice these things over and over again even though the wording isn't exactly the same. It isn't a verbatim script. It was something you worked with mentally so that it came out quickly and succinctly, but you didn't really think a lot about it." An effective message must appear natural. Even if you choose to use a script or notes, make it your own and the client will want to engage with you.

If we do not consider the client's position or think about the environment our message may create, we might prepare the wrong message. As an example of messaging run amok, Mike Bradley tells a cautionary story. Mike is general manager of Derse Exhibits Pittsburgh and a vice president of the parent corporation, which designs and creates trade show exhibits. One time, Mike joined a new company as a salesperson and early on said to the chief marketing officer (CMO), "If I'm a new sales prospect and I'm interested in understanding more about this company, what are our sales aids? What do we have to tell our story?"

The CMO showed Mike the company's 250-slide Power-Point presentation. The show included a history of the company—material with virtually no relevance to any prospect thinking of buying the company's products. It talked about the dedicated company employees, prizes the firm had won, top management background, client list, and the number and location of offices around the country. Mike said to the CMO, "You have to be kidding me. You want someone to sit through 250 slides and hope that buried somewhere in there is something a client might be interested in? No way."

Mike believes that, unfortunately, many sales organizations still operate as though the company's own history, accomplishments, and successes are relevant to outsiders. "Not organizations driven by sales, but in some driven by the marketing staff. I think sales effectiveness is a combination of the relationship and the proper tools to help the salesperson tell the story. By the time I made my first presentation, the 250 slides were down to 18. Selling is all about knowing that customer as well as you possibly can and what is most likely to interest him before you

58

even walk in the door, particularly for a formal presentation." Not only was Mike thinking like a buyer, his mind-set that messaging is important drove him to make these changes in the presentation.

Use words that will resonate with your client. This includes questions. Think of the questions you need to ask and what you wish to gain by the discussion before you meet a prospective customer. Create a preface for each question that is comfortable for you and for the prospect, such as "Do you mind if I ask . . . ?" Or, "Is this a good time to talk about . . . ?" Through establishing your intent, planning your questions and content, and creating an atmosphere conducive to trust and rapport, you will communicate a highly effective message, one that causes the customer to want to know more.

Occasionally a salesperson will say to me, "I worry about my messaging. I have the knowledge and I'm building the relationships [or I have the relationships], but people just don't want to listen to me."

I ask the person, "Why do you think that's true? Tell me how you message. Give me an example of what you say to people when you meet them." Most salespeople in their messaging sound like a salesperson: "I would like to talk to you today about . . ." or "Have you ever thought about . . . ?" When you sound like a typical salesperson (too scripted), the person you are talking to almost always behaves like a buyer. That's the first problem, and it's big one.

The second is that if your messaging isn't very good, you may be overestimating your ability to build relationships. If your relationship—the trust and rapport you have—is strong, some people will make allowances for weaker messaging. Every salesperson ought to learn that without meaningful dialogue, there is no selling. There may be buying, but there will be no selling.

Effective messaging means engaging in a meaningful dialogue. I define *meaningful dialogue* as an adult discussion of the truth. My business partner Mike MacLeod defines it as a free flow of meaning. In both definitions, it means a conversation—two people talking. It is not a monologue. It is not one person talking and the other barely listening.

The key here is that your words matter in triggering the dialogue, and you have to believe that. Yet, when I sit in on a sales call, I almost always hear the salesperson say things that probably could be said much more effectively. Average salespeople have not given as much thought to the words they employ as they should. They may not blurt things out, but it often seems they do not plan as thoroughly as they could for the precise words that will make their story come to life and create energy.

Law of Sales Intent Number 7 says, "I intend to use words and find language that will resonate with my prospects and will be compelling." When we consistently say the right thing at the right time in the right way, we are more persuasive, we sell more, and we are more effective. But what is the right thing? How do you get to the point where your words consistently have the effect you want?

When it comes to a sales message, the right thing is driven by a combination of the *right* intent (discussed earlier) and the *right* content, a combination that is best accomplished by thinking like a buyer and not like a seller.

Most salespeople intend to be truthful; very few lie outright. But even though what we say is true, something less than 100 percent of what we say is believable in the eyes of the customer or prospect. Take it one step farther; something less than 100 percent of what is believable is also compelling. An easy way to see how much of what you say is compelling is to look at your market share: Wherever people are buying, you are compelling.

Words matter! They create impact, and consequently if you prepare your words for every call with that as a mind-set, you'll make far more sales. Your message is not about your product or service but an attempt to learn if there is a fit between your offer and the customer's needs. What should you say on this encounter, and how predictable is the encounter likely to be? If it's predictable, you ought to spend enough time to figure out the most compelling thing to say. Too often, however, salespeople are not prepared to make their questions, their stories, and their examples as powerful as they could be because they don't torture every single word.

This is not the way most of us ordinarily operate, so it is necessary to practice. It is almost like improvisational theater. The actors have a situation and usually a character; they have to invent lines that fit the character and advance the situation. When you watch the great improvisational actors, they look natural. They seem natural and unrehearsed but it is because they have rehearsed. Perhaps they have not rehearsed this exact situation and character, but they have practiced hundreds of others so they are prepared. When you internalize ideas through extensive rehearsal, the concepts are no longer words on paper but thoughts in your head that you have translated into effective communications.

Salespeople need to think not only about the information they seek through their questions, but also about the atmosphere, the climate, and the mood they hope to create with the words they use. Select the right words to create a positive mood, movement, atmosphere, climate, and feeling. Only by thinking through comprehensively can you select the right words, thus creating an effective message.

If you want the customer to buy, a two-way conversation must occur. Too often, sales calls don't encourage meaningful dialogue and salespeople get passive listening—if that. The salesperson is usually advancing the major concepts and the major hypothesis and does most of the talking. But you want the other person to respond actively. Keep your mind focused on the other person and on having a conversation by using the right words and listening. When you prepare for this level of interaction, you will most likely make the sale. If all you get is passive listening to your monologue—no matter how polished it may be—you are not likely to make a sale.

THE RELATIONSHIP MIND-SET: THE WAY YOU CONNECT

The third leg to this stool we've been building is the relationship. Your relationship mind-set must be that building relationships is important to you. If you don't believe that a positive business relationship with prospects and customers is important, you are not going to make the effort (and it *is* an effort) to build one.

Most people in business understand that positive business relationships can help them do their jobs. Most salespeople know that they are more successful with customers with whom they have a good business relationship. In fact, the more good relationships you have and the more diverse those relationships, the more effective you can be at whatever you do.

Most of us take an accidental or reactive approach to building relationships. We tend to just let them happen. A more effective life and professional strategy is to build relationships strategically, not because you want to make a lot of money (although that doesn't hurt) or be successful on whatever terms are meaningful to you, but because you want to have a more fulfilling and rewarding life. In many ways, the quantity and the quality of your relationships determine the quality of your life.

Most people build their relationships haphazardly. If you have the relationship mind-set that relationships are important, you should consciously, deliberately, and strategically map your relationships (we call this *relationship mapping*) with four groups of people:

1. *People within the organization who are important to your success:* You need these people to get your job done. They may include customer service reps, warehouse clerks, finance people—everyone who can make your work easier . . . or impossible. They should be a diverse group, not simply your peers in sales, but colleagues from many parts of the organization. The more diverse they are, the better.

2. *People external to the organization who are important to getting your job done:* They may be customers, vendors, regulators, anybody—but they are not within the walls of your company.

3. *People who are important to the success of your career:* These could include your boss, the human resource

director, a mentor, or someone else within the company. You need to meet and develop a relationship with these people if they can help you either understand something about a future opportunity or help you find an opportunity. They may also be outside the company—coaches, friends, or a spouse. They are people who will share their insights and experiences, tell you when they believe you are making a mistake, or suggest options that you otherwise may never consider.

4. *People with whom you need to repair a relationship:* You know them—they are the customers (or ex-customers) you or the organization have alienated (usually not intentionally) that you'd like to improve your relationship with, or *must* improve your relationship with to do your job effectively. You may be lucky and have no one in this group, but these people probably exist even if you can't identify them, and you are much more likely to be successful if you are clear about who they are.

The goal of relationship building is to understand and persuade the other person to listen to you differently by establishing yourself as unique, trustworthy, credible, and consummate professional. You will, after all, get everything in life you want if you help other people get what they want, and you will have more fun. Therefore, your relationship building does not have to be targeted toward attaining specific actions on the part of another person.

Also remember that everybody is important (the Shari Kulkis credo); there are no "little people." I cringe when I hear someone use that phrase. They tend to mean the janitors, the file clerks, receptionists, the administrative staff; they're not talking about management. Whenever people have that attitude, they almost see others as part of a caste system, and that is a destructive mind-set.

A mind-set that relationship building is an investment over the long haul pays dividends in the short term as well as the long haul. People say to me, "You keep talking about this relationship building, but it takes so long to do." The point I make is that it doesn't take long to build a relationship with everybody and you begin to gain the benefits of a relationship the moment you start focusing on other people.

The minute you focus on other people, you find that more people like you, more people want to do things for you, they want to listen to you, and that's not long term; that's right now. But if you are selfish and think that building a relationship is too much of a long-term project, you are not likely to do it—and you are not going to get any results.

Unfortunately, few of us know how to consciously, systematically, and routinely build and maintain positive business relationships. Most of us cannot build a positive business relationship from scratch with someone who is key to our business success, nor do we know how to improve a relationship that has been going nowhere, change a relationship in which the other person does not like us, or develop a positive relationship that is adversarial by its nature.

Positive relationships are the basic unit of every business—positive relationships with customers, suppliers, and employees. Businesses such as management consultants, accountants, and lawyers depend more heavily on personal relationships with their customers than others. At the same time, relationships with other people are important to every business, and the more complex the sale and the issue, the more important the relationship.

If you have superior relationships with customers and prospects, you will, almost automatically, be more successful, assuming you also have the necessary knowledge and messaging skills. Certainly the converse is true: When you have poor relationships with customers, your business life suffers (not to mention your personal life).

The key words here are *consciously, systematically,* and *routinely.* Building positive business relationships is a skill anyone can learn. It requires a process you can master because you already know instinctively what the process requires. Adopt the simple steps I discuss in detail in Chapter 9 and your business (and personal) relationships will improve.

Your relationship affects how much and how well the customer or prospect wants to listen to you. The quality of your business is a function of your ability to get other people to want to have conversations with you. If the relationship is good, the other person will value your message, knowing that you would not share the information if you did not think it would be valuable. Prospects and customers (like everyone) take into account not only what is being said but who is saying it. You have a much greater chance to persuade when other people feel positive toward you than when they are indifferent or negative.

When you have a good relationship, your rapport, trust, and respect are instantly evident. This enables you to have a meaningful dialogue far more often than otherwise. Such an adult conversation rooted in the truth can only occur when there is a strong, positive relationship between two people. It is the relationship's strength that makes the dialogue possible, and it's the relationship that helps you navigate the rough waters as well.

Anthony Yim says that in his early days of selling telecommunications equipment and services, he happened to read a *Time* magazine article about a famous Wall Street mover and shaker who had quit his company to start a financial trading firm. The executive had a huge vision and big plans. "It was in my sales territory," says Anthony, "but I shared the territory with other sales reps. I researched it because it was coming into my territory and because it sounded cool—different from what I usually did."

Anthony researched the executive, his new company, and the industry to bring himself up to speed on what the firm was trying to do and the trials it faced. One day, Anthony finally learned exactly where the firm planned to headquarter the new business—in a town near his office. He began visiting the company and eventually met the person in charge of the telecommunications function. "We were the underdog," says Anthony, "but because I had thought about this guy's business for a couple of months, I had visualized having it. When we met, I believe he sensed I knew more and cared more about their business than the other sales reps. All that helped to build our relationship, and we eventually won their business, which was to connect their offices overseas."

Then the network that Anthony's company maintained across the Atlantic Ocean went down. The backup network was only about 30 percent effective, so Anthony's new customer had a huge loss in their service quality. "My competitor, who was much bigger than my company and had lost the contract, was in their office every day," says Anthony. "But I was there, too. Because we had done a good job, and hadn't done a hard sell in the beginning—we cared, we listened, we wanted to do what was right, and we continued to support them—the other guys were not able to take over the account."

Because Anthony demonstrated that he had learned the firm's business, he had built a strong relationship. "I would go in and get a tour of every last piece of equipment they ever bought. I would have the executive in charge explain every single thing he did and why he did it. I was interested, although sometimes it got to be a little bit too much. But, by being there and letting that executive be himself and be important, he was able to defend us to his bosses to give us more time."

After three and a half weeks, Anthony's company was able to repair the network problem and gave the customer a credit for the lost service. "The reality is we put a little hurt on them. Thankfully, they stuck with us, and it showed me that if you don't build the relationship properly in the beginning, if there's no trust, or if the level of trust isn't really high, or if there's no sense that you care about the customer—if they sense you care more about their ability to pay you than what they are doing and how you can help—then you are always at risk. People understand people make mistakes and if you build the relationship they are willing to give that extra slack. I was promoted and left my position after about a year and a half. I turned the business over to another salesperson, who grew it into an enormous account. But if we not had a good relationship in the beginning, there would have been no account to grow."

Sean Feeney, the CEO and president of Inovis, says that his company analyzes every lost deal. Inovis provides software network and synchronization services that essentially help major retailers and manufacturers get their orders to vendors right—ideally, orders with no mistakes. Sean says, "The number one reason we lose a deal to someone is because either they had a better relationship or we had no previous relationship with them. We spend an awful lot of time working on having a relationship, and very often the hard part for companies and for salespeople is building the relationship over time when the deal is way off in the future. With more and more pressure to perform quarter-to-quarter, it gets tougher and tougher to build a relationship and trust over time. We see that time and time again."

Both Anthony and Sean tell stories about the power of business relationships in achieving success. They also depict the importance of preparation and time in building relationships. Anthony's success was directly related to the homework he did prior to meeting with the company. His knowledge, which was above and beyond the average, enabled him to build a solid relationship that endured through the rough spots. That's the beauty of a strong business relationship. Sean talks about the concept of building the relationship before the business occurs. His success is in the preparation. A mind-set that sees the crucial importance of long-term relationship building is obviously beneficial. Only when you have this mind-set will you invest in the relationship the way you should.

BUILD CONFIDENCE AND PASSION

Here are two other related benefits. If you are very good at messaging because you have great knowledge, and if you are good at building relationships, having the combination of these skills gives you confidence.

Confidence is an intangible that will increase your effectiveness spectacularly. It enables you to actually practice the principle that the less you care about the sale the more you sell. You really don't care, because you are prepared for anything, and if this product or service or proposal isn't right for this prospect, that's fine. There are other prospects.

The second benefit is that when you have knowledge and it leads you to a position where you believe ardently in the product or service you are offering *and* you are good at messaging and relationship building, not only do you have confidence, but you are also likely to have passion for what you are doing. Most customers respond positively to salespeople who have a passion for what they sell. If you want to test this, visit an Apple Computer store to talk with a salesperson; every one I've met has been a raging fan of the products and that passion comes through in the way they talk to customers.

There is no more powerful combination in selling than extensive knowledge, good messaging, and positive business relationships—these lead to confidence and passion, and drive effective communication. Don't make the mistake of focusing on one or two of these elements as if they were stand-alone issues. Again, the three are interdependent. They are inextricably interwoven—one impacts the other and the other and the other. There is nothing more potent than professionals who are confident and passionate about who they are and what they represent.

Now, lets talk about some tested techniques and a process to **D**evelop customer interest, **E**ngage in a meaningful dialogue, **L**earn the situation, **T**ell your story, and **A**sk for a commitment (the DELTA process).

SECTION II

USE A
TESTED, EFFECTIVE
SALES PROCESS

CHAPTER 4

DEVELOP INTEREST SO CUSTOMERS WILL HEAR YOU

While any number of good sales processes exist and work well, we have developed one based on the acronym DELTA that is particularly effective. We like it because it means change. And change is the ultimate objective of all sales conversations. It is relatively simple, can be adapted to virtually any industry or sales situation, and works most effectively with the other two keys to sales success, mind-set and relationship building. The five steps in the DELTA acronym are Develop, Engage, Learn, Tell, and Ask:

1. *D*evelop prospective customers' interest so they are willing to hear you out.

2. *E*ngage customers in a meaningful dialogue.

3. *L*earn the prospect's situation/problem/challenge.

4. *T*ell your story after you understand clearly that your product or service is a fit for their situation, problem, or challenge.

5. *A*sk for a commitment, when a commitment is appropriate.

Because these topics are so significant, each one has its own chapter. And I start where every sales conversation must start, by developing the prospect's interest in what you have to say.

YOUR FIRST WORDS MATTER MOST

If it is true that people develop their impression of us in the first 30 to 60 seconds and that impression is lasting, then your first words—whether this is the first time you've ever interacted with the person or the fiftieth—still really matter. The traditional, "How's it going?" or "How was your weekend?" are not overly compelling ways to begin the conversation. This bland, generic opening may be acceptable if you have a great relationship with the person and are 100 percent certain that your question will be immediately recognized as sincere. If so, the person knows you really want to know how their weekend turned out. But as a rule, "How's it going?" or "How's business?" does not develop anybody's interest.

It is critical to understand the importance of your first words and plan what you are going to say. If you have learned something interesting and relevant to the customer's situation, how are you going to introduce it? You want to use first words that you have researched, planned carefully, and that create interest because you want the person to react by saying, "Wow, I didn't know that. That's interesting." You want this because your first words often determine whether the customer or prospect wants to extend the interaction or end it.

There are five key principles to developing a prospective customer's interest:

1. Research to find interesting things to open the dialogue.
2. Use openings that create safe environments.
3. Bring value to the interaction before you start the sales conversation.
4. Make connections that can help the customer/prospect.
5. Be crystal clear about what you need to know and go about finding that out.

But how, exactly, do you put these principles into daily practice?

RESEARCH TO FIND INTERESTING THINGS TO OPEN THE DIALOGUE

It is self-evident that if people don't want to listen to you, you aren't going to sell them anything. If they don't want to listen, they simply will not hear the most powerful, valuable, significant sales story in the world. You first have to make people want to listen.

Making people want to listen is a function of how much you know, how well you present what you know, how creative you are in shaping what you say, how much time you spend planning for a sales conversation, and how much genuine interest you convey in your dialogue with prospects and customers.

One way to begin is by saying something unique, interesting, and relevant that the prospect didn't know. You can do some research on the Internet to learn things people ordinarily wouldn't know but would find intriguing. If you were selling anything to do with sleep—mattresses, white noise machines, light-blocking window treatments, medications—prospects might be interested in knowing the two developments that profoundly changed human sleep patterns that had been relatively unchanged for thousands of years: the invention of the alarm clock by Levi Hutchins, a Concord, New Hampshire, clockmaker in 1787, and the invention of the first commercially successful incandescent lamp by Thomas Edison around 1879.

If you are selling a drug for depression and you say to a physician who treats depression, "I have been doing some research on the Internet and I was fascinated to learn who is considered the father of depression. Is that something they taught you in medical school, by chance?" The average doctor is going to say, "No, who is it?" and you have developed interest with that factoid. (It was John Burton who wrote a paper in 1650, "The Art of Melancholia," and became the first person to coin the term *depression*.)

The crucial point here is that the unique factoid ought to be interesting to the customer, not something the person probably already knows, and it should be relevant. You should not go in and ask, "Do you know who won the Super Bowl in 1967?" That's not a good idea because it is probably irrelevant to the prospect and your sales message. (If it's clearly relevant, that's different.) If I were selling copying machines, I would want to know the first person to come up with the idea to copy something mechanically. If I were selling fax machines, I would want to know that the first patent for a fax was granted in 1843.

If I were selling computers, I would want to understand the Bill Gates story thoroughly. Gates, arguably, the one person most responsible for personal computers, became rich, not only because he was smart, but because of his mother. I would want to be able to tell his story because it would likely create interest. Lots of people don't know that three of the four wealthiest people in the country didn't finish college. Bill Gates didn't finish college; Larry Ellison of Oracle didn't finish college, and Paul Allen of Charter Communications didn't finish college.

When you say something prospects or customers probably don't know but can relate to your product or service (or the condition it addresses), they will usually find that informative. If they do know that Levi Hutchins invented the first alarm clock, they may well be proud to demonstrate their knowledge. Do some research on your own. Use the Internet to find facts/statistics/trivia on the prospect's industry or business. Share something that includes an interesting and relevant fact that you can relate to your product (preferably present it in a creative way). Another form of research is to ask for their opinion or feedback about a relevant issue that you can relate to your product in a safe environment. Asking their opinion almost always secures interest because most people like to give their opinion. The key is to ensure prospective customers do not feel you are asking because you intend to use their response to "sell" them.

When I tell people they have to say something interesting, they often think they have to entertain or say something novel and unique, but that is not necessarily the case. You can be interesting without being entertaining. If people believe you are genuinely interested in them, they are usually interested in you. Your interest will generate theirs, and the fact that you have done your research says a lot about how you approach business.

USE OPENINGS THAT CREATE SAFE ENVIRONMENTS

Far too many salespeople begin a meeting by signaling *"This is a sales call."* They use traditional and easily recognized sales language: "Today I would like to talk to you about . . ." or "Have you ever thought about . . ." or, in a retail store, "Can I help you?" or, on the phone, "If I could save you money on your long distance calls, would you be interested?" All such phrases signal to prospects that this is about to be a stereotypical sales inter-action: "I want to talk to you about my product or service and hope you'll buy it." That does not create a safe environment, nor is it likely to create interest. It puts the prospect on guard and hy-persensitive to any sales pressure.

Whenever I call on prospects or clients, I start my part of the sales conversation by saying, "We do business with a lot of com-panies and we are proud of our work, but that doesn't mean we are right for you. At the end of the day, the only way I will know whether our offering is a fit for what you are trying to do is to understand more about your situation. Before I launch into how great we are, can I ask you a few questions?" Everyone to whom I've ever said this has answered, "Yes, go right ahead."

I usually start with the question, "Tell me how you landed in this position" because I want them to talk about how they got their current title. What assignments did they have before? In response, some people will tell you their life story. Others will just say something like, "Well, I used to be the district manager in Dallas, and now I am the regional manager in Birmingham."

To keep the conversation going, I usually say, "Tell me a lit-tle bit about your responsibilities and what you do." After they tell me what they do, I say, "Tell me what you are trying to ac-complish in [the specific area in which we probably have a mu-tual interest]."

Whether you have one person or six people in the room, they will usually allow you to ask questions. You are there to help them, but to do so you have to understand their situation. What creates the interest is your obvious objectivity, because you signal with your opening words that you are not sure whether you are right for them. That you are doing business with companies they recognize is all they must know to accept that you have a credible offering. It does not mean that what you have is the right offering for them—and you acknowledge that—but the fact that it's right for somebody gives you the ticket to get inside the tent.

Valerie Sokolosky at Valerie & Company says that the first thing she does when calling a potential client (and she always makes the initial contact by phone) is to build rapport by asking simple questions: "Why don't you tell me about yourself?" "How long have you been at the company?" "Oh, you must have seen a lot of changes." She wants to convey her interest before she even attempts to learn the organization's issues.

"If I can't make the customer feel like I care about him or her first," says Valerie, "I won't get their heart. Does the client feel I have their best interests at heart? I am on the phone because I think I have a service that will help them but I always say, 'Before I explore the needs of your organization, tell me a little bit about you and your involvement with the organization.' I also let them know right up front, that I may or may not be the right resource, but that's why I'm calling, to explore that with them."

Valerie says she seldom loses a sale if the client recognizes the need. "A client just told me, 'Thank you for being so responsive,' because I called back when I said I would. She said she thought I would enjoy speaking at their conference because I would fit in. To me she was saying, not that I did a great job selling, but that she felt I was real; I wasn't trying to sell her unless my services met her needs. By the time the rapport has been built—and that's number one—and they believe and trust that my credibility and expertise is what they are looking for—and that's number two—it automatically leads to a close. I don't have to push for a close."

What does Valerie do in the increasingly common situation of being handed off to, or having to go through, an executive's administrative assistant? She says that if the assistant is really trying to help the boss and has an open mind, that's great. "However, you can run into a person who is taken with her authority and comes back to you with something like, 'Well, I'm just looking into a lot of different companies. We have to explore a lot of different people. We have to compare your prices to someone else's.' Which is an immediate clue that they are not looking for the expert, they are looking for price."

If you get that, says Valerie, you have to realize that, unless you can get past her, the assistant is going to be a gatekeeper and certainly not an advocate. "If you don't have the person's heart, she won't want to keep listening to you. If you are just another number, no matter who you are or what you say, there is nothing you can do. You can do everything right, and there is a wall. And if you can't break it down, you can't break it down."

Another way to treat this situation is to treat the gatekeeper as the client. When she realizes you are different and that you will create the same safe environment with her supervisor, you are liable to go further faster.

In most sales situations, there is naturally some pressure; you want prospects to act or think in a way they may not have considered completely. The whole concept of creating a safe environment is intended to take as much pressure off customers as possible so they can listen to what you are saying and think clearly about what you are offering. We begin to do that (usually) when we signal that this is a *sales conversation,* not a sales call. In a sales conversation, two (or more) people are having a meaningful dialogue about real issues and concerns. They are

82

trying to learn something important from each other that they can both use to improve their situations. Conversely, in a traditional sales call a salesperson is attempting to obtain an order.

Most people do not want to have a conversation with someone they perceive as being single-minded about trying to sell them something, whether it is a product, a service, or an ideology. Many people, however, will have a conversation with someone who may be selling something, but takes an approach that says in effect, "If it meets your needs [or solves your problem] you'll buy it. But if it's not in your best interest to buy it, then it's okay to tell me no. And I'm not going to pressure you to make a decision one way or another." The less pressure you put on customers, the more likely you are to open up their minds to new possibilities, possibilities that include your product or service.

One of the best ways to start removing pressure is with the way you craft your questions. Typically, salespeople are taught to ask questions that elicit a "Yes," response. In fact, some authors argue that sales reps should make it easy for people to say "Yes." These books teach reps to start by asking questions in such a way that prospects grow accustomed to saying "Yes," so that by the end, they'll say "Yes" to the order.

I disagree. I believe that great salespeople (those who understand how important it is to take pressure off the customer or prospect) do exactly the opposite. Great salespeople make it easy for prospects or customers to say "No."

By asking questions that make it easy for customers to say, "No," great salespeople create a safe environment around which to continue building the relationship. A simple example: Every time I telephone somebody for a business reason, I first ask, "Is

83

now a good time to talk?" I make it easy for them to tell me, "No."

If they say "Yes," then they have given me permission to have the dialogue, and I know they are willing to hear me out. I do the same thing when I am following up with somebody who has told me they want me to contact them in a month. I send them an e-mail or leave a message saying, "You asked me to follow up; I don't know what your situation is now, or whether your priorities have changed or not, or whether you are still interested in this or not, but if you are, give me a call."

That message contains two or three excuses clients can play back to me ("Our priorities haven't changed; we are still interested; call next month"). I am signaling to them some ways that they can nicely tell me "No." In response, they sense that I am not applying pressure in any way, and when they say "Yes," they mean it.

Look at this simple question, "Would you prefer to meet on Thursday or Friday?"

In typical sales situations, people have been trained to ask questions like these (a forced choice) to encourage prospects to choose a day that guarantees the appointment. It leaves no "out" for them. Most people immediately feel pressure when you put them in this situation. If they feel pressure before the appointment, how do you think your meeting will go if you get the appointment? Are they likely to be open to listening to you, or will they feel they have to be on guard against further pressure?

Here is a different way to ask that same question: "Let's look at our calendars together. My calendar is fairly open. What days this week would be good for you?" Or, if you are traveling to their area, "I am going to be in town the week of the 15th.

What day that week looks like it might work for you since I have some flexibility in my schedule?"

Asking either question gives clients an out or an opportunity to say "No day would be good." No forced choice, but no pressure either. By using these words, you create an open and positive psychological state in which prospects do not feel they are being cornered. If they take the meeting, they are more likely to be interested in hearing how you might help them than if you had forced the issue, even subtly.

Rich Harshaw at Y2 Marketing, a Grapevine, Texas, marketing consulting firm, goes even further. He almost makes it hard for prospects to say "Yes." Here, from a training recording Harshaw uses for his staff, is an excerpt from a sales call with a real estate executive who had developed a software product he wanted to sell. The prospect wanted a marketing company that could present some packaging options. Harshaw states to the prospect right up front, "I'm just going to tell you this as plainly as I know how. Hopefully, this doesn't offend you. Any dumbass can come up with a logo and a color. But here's the key: What the hell do you do with that stuff?"

The client responds, "You need to have the product in a cover—in a CD sleeve. You need to sell the product."

Harshaw says, "No one gives a damn what the CD sleeve looks like. . . . Holy crap, man, we're going to put all of this attention into building an identity that no one's going to freaking see until they've bought it.

"Hey . . . Rich, you need to tone it down some. We're trying to be professional here. Back off a little bit."

"I don't care if we get this deal or not. But if you are going to buy into an ad agency that's going to put together this logo-identity package, I already know what happens. You get high expectations because this stuff looks cool. And it doesn't [sell]. I've seen it happen so many times, it makes my stomach turn. It makes me want to vomit."

Harshaw agrees he is aggressive, but he is convinced that not every potential client is ready for what Y2 Marketing offers. "Our company is more interested in converts than clients," says Edward Earle, the company's president. And although this real estate executive did not buy Y2's services (while many others have), Harshaw says that in retrospect he would do nothing differently. "Any business has got to have the faith that there are enough customers out there that can think this way. There's no reason to get hung up on one account."[1]

This is not a technique I would recommend for everyone because you might come across as arrogant and condescending. Although at first glance, Harshaw's approach seems to contradict my view that you want to create a safe environment for prospects and customers, it actually does create a safe environment. It telegraphs that brutal honesty is fine in this sales conversation. That can be very helpful in certain situations with certain customers. The truth rarely comes out unless the environment is safe, no matter how it is created.

BRING VALUE BEFORE YOU START TO SELL

The other thing to do is to share things with customers and prospects that can help them even before your first meeting. There are many ways to bring value; but you need to make it a habit and not an afterthought.

For example, you have read in the newspaper that a prospective client company is having difficulty with its margins and you have just read a great book on how to raise an organization's margins without changing the culture. One way to bring value before your meeting is to send the book with a note: "I saw in the paper that one of the issues you are trying to address is margins and I thought you might like to see this book." It's the concept of an inexpensive, unexpected, thoughtful item that they would treasure, done before you know for certain what they treasure but not before you know what's important to them.

If I know that one of my clients is looking for a new head of training, I can bring value by suggesting people I think could fill the job. If I know they are looking for a secretary, a janitor, or somebody to keep the books part time, I will try to make that connection for them. Doctors always struggle with how to deal with managed care. Any article or book on how to improve quality at the point of care and do it in less time has value to physician customers. The item you provide before you meet with them will likely be appreciated and make them want to talk with you. It could be about the business or about their personal life—anything that is an issue for them.

I had a meeting with a potential client who is in charge of sales force effectiveness for an organization that has 5,000 salespeople. I was not there to sell him. I had met him once, and he told me what he did. I told him what we did, and he said his company had started a sales effectiveness improvement process about six weeks earlier. He said he would be grateful if I came in and looked at what they were doing to see if I thought they were leaving anything out of the process. I said I'd be glad to.

I extended another business trip to spend an hour and a half with him, and when we met, I said, "Take me through what you're doing." I made notes while he was talking, and when he was finished, I said: "When your people come back to you with their recommendations, just make sure this is there, and this, and this, and this."

During our conversation, he tried to get me to sell him on the services my company offers. I told him, "I don't want to have that discussion with you." He wanted to know why not. "Trust me, if you decide to go down that road with us, we can do it in a manner consistent with the way your organization functions. But I wouldn't have the discussion if I were you unless and until your organization identifies it as a need. If they identify it as a need, then you and I can have the discussion. If they don't identify it as one of their pressing needs, you need to ask, why isn't it? They've either got a good answer or they don't, but you have to make that decision. But talk to me about the issues where you think we can help only after you've concluded from the research your organization is doing that there is a need."

I told him he needed to get buy-in from the organization, which is exactly what he was doing. The organization was going to come back and tell him the problems and how to solve them. His job as the executive leading the project was to ensure the organization was asking all the right questions. I tried to give him some thoughts on questions that my experience told me they might overlook. I said he would have to introduce those ideas into the discussion, but he would still have to let the salespeople decide the right way to deal with them from the options available.

He said, "I'm just anticipating what they're going to come back with."

I said, "Don't anticipate. Wait until they come back with something, and then if they identify a need for the things we do, and if you want to have a dialogue with us, that's the time to do it." I was looking for a way to bring value to him without trying to sell anything, and indeed, I have no idea whether we are going to sell him anything.

He tried to turn our conversation into a sales call and I wouldn't let him because it wasn't right. Had I allowed him to turn our meeting into a sales call, I would not be practicing what I'm preaching. He has not established that the organization wants to teach their salespeople how to build better business relationships. He believes it is important, but if the organization doesn't believe it, any training will fail no matter how valuable I think it would be.

If nothing else, I've changed a contact into a friend, and if our stuff fits, his organization will come to that conclusion without my telling him. But they'll come to that conclusion in part because of the value I created for him by offering him my expertise on the subject of sales force effectiveness.

If he calls me, we'll have a meaningful dialogue. I'll go from the macro to the micro: how many salespeople . . . how often they meet together . . . how much distance learning they do . . . how they use training . . . what role the training folks play . . . who's going to be the decision maker. That's where I learn about the exact situation, problem, or challenge.

There are many ways to bring value to your customers, but you've got to make it a habit and not an afterthought. If you give people a thought or an idea that can help them, you never lose—

as long as you are careful not to be an industry gossip. Giving value requires you to do research to find something not only interesting to them but also important to them. If you can find something important to them, it's a lot easier to find something they will find valuable. You can read up on the company on the Internet and pay attention to what is being said about the company in the business press. It might not be a company problem; it might be an industry problem. The airline industry may be struggling with supply chain, but you learn the medical device business has developed systems around supply chain, so you can point out that while this is a different industry, some of the ideas can apply.

MAKE CONNECTIONS THAT CAN HELP THE CUSTOMER

You can develop interest by connecting people to other people. Say something like this: "You know I was driving down the road the other day and I was thinking about you, and I was thinking you ought to meet so and so, because . . ." You are sincerely trying to help them; you're not trying to be manipulative.

People find that interesting because it goes back to one of the fundamental facts of human beings. People want to associate with people who can help them in some aspect of their life. So if you are thinking about how you create interest for people, ask yourself how you can help them in some aspect of their life. One way may be to help prospects connect with three groups of people with whom you may already have a connection:

1. *People within the organization who are important to the customer's success:* These are the people who can help

customers do their jobs. They may include customer service reps, warehouse clerks, finance people—everyone who can make your work easier . . . or impossible. Sometimes, I've found, an outsider may be able to see—and assist in building—relationships that people inside the organization either do not see or, for political reasons, cannot make the first move.

2. *People external to the organization who are important to the customer's achievements:* They could be anybody, but they are not within the walls of the customer's company. These could be other vendors, consultants, or trade press reporters.

3. *People who are important to the success of customer's career:* These may be contacts you have within the customer's company or in other organizations. They are people who will share their insights and experiences.

Henry Potts is the national sales manager for Melillo Consulting, in Somerset, New Jersey. Melillo is a business and technology systems integrator and reseller of Hewlett-Packard products; he points out that it is critical in his business to understand the relationship of the person within the organization he is calling on. "There are so many levels in an organization and your questions need to be based upon the level of the person you are talking to and what you already potentially know about the work they do. That is something that you have to be careful of or sensitive to when you go into an account. If, for example, I am talking to a person in information technology operations at a first line manager level, my value proposition should not be around reducing costs in operations or in reducing the number of people in his organization. You have to line up with what that individual's interests are. If I was talking to his boss, or the chief information technology officer, who has that problem in the overall budget, I am going to be talking to him in a different way. And asking different sorts of questions."

He adds, "it is very important before you start the dialogue to have an understanding of the organization. A key component of planning for the call is to have an understanding of the position the person has in the organization and what typically might be their motivators." This kind of understanding helps you determine what connection you could make that might be meaningful to prospects, individually and organizationally.

BE CLEAR ABOUT WHAT YOU NEED TO KNOW

If you want to enhance and make the sales interaction successful—and indeed be seen as different from all other salespeople—you need to be prepared in two ways: in the *content* and in the *condition* of the call. The content consists of all the things you are ready to ask about, learn about, and discuss.

The condition is the psychological environment—or emotional mood—you create that can successfully differentiate you from other salespeople and rapidly make the customer want this interaction to occur and possibly to extend the interaction. The goal is to establish and sustain a low-pressure environment through relationship building and credible messaging.

You should prepare the content of every sales conversation by asking yourself: What do I want to know and what do I want to share? You need to be prepared to discuss information about yourself, your product, your services, and your industry.

By preparing your words and your actions carefully, you create an environment in which someone wants to respond. Where trust and rapport are strong, selling pressure will seem weak. This environment is what I refer to as your condition—creating psychological safety for the prospect. From the moment you begin to speak, the condition you create either makes or does not make the other person comfortable. When prospects are comfortable, they feel at ease and open to conversation.

The condition of the call is important whenever you are trying to persuade, influence, or sell. You want prospects and customers to feel they can tell you the truth and can talk about their real challenges because they believe you want to help. (At the same time, prospects always understand that if they buy what you're selling, they're helping you as well.)

You want to develop interest, to encourage people to listen to you, not because you are an appointment in a busy day but because what you have to say is both interesting and potentially valuable. The quality of your business is directly linked to the desire of your customers to have a conversation with you and that is linked to the way you develop interest.

You develop interest partly by building the relationship, partly by understanding whether to go from a personal discussion to a business discussion. It requires knowing far more about the customer than the average salesperson so you can say something interesting that makes the customer want to listen to you.

To successfully manage the content and the condition of the call, you must focus on building the business relationship while selling your product. The stronger your relationship, the easier it is to create the conditions under which you can accurately assess the content (and the more difficult it is for another salesperson to poach on your territory).

In the selling world, a balance of strong content and safe conditions creates the greatest likelihood for potential success because people buy with emotion and justify the purchase with reason. So the condition you want to create in the call is more about emotion than logic. The more open and honest that environment can be, the greater the chance that your listeners will hear your arguments with an open mind.

It may take a long time for you to craft the exact language to create the optimal content and condition for your call, but it will increase your effectiveness as a salesperson. Think about and plan for both as you prepare your first words. You will have far more valuable and successful sales interactions. Because you have developed interest from the beginning, your customers and prospects will want to hear more from you, not see less of you. They will in fact be disposed to engage in a meaningful dialogue with you.

CHAPTER 5

ENGAGE CUSTOMERS IN MEANINGFUL DIALOGUE

These next two steps in the DELTA process—*E*ngage customers and *L*earn their situation—are interconnected. One flows into the other and, in fact, they can take place simultaneously. But I find it useful to speak about them separately because, in general, we must first engage customers in a meaningful dialogue before we are likely to learn their situation. Without meaningful dialogue, there may be order taking but no sales conversation. Indeed, without meaningful dialogue, a salesperson cannot help a customer buy.

Meaningful dialogue, as I said earlier, is an adult discussion of the truth or a free flow of meaning. In both definitions, it means a conversation, a back-and-forth interchange between two people talking. It is not one person talking and the other listening politely. It is having a meaningful conversation with customers about their companies, their industry, or themselves.

Meaningful dialogue is a powerful concept and is likely to happen consistently only when our knowledge is broad and our relationship with the customer solid. In a meaningful dialogue, the client feels safe, and you can have open and honest two-way communication, which may lead to the customer buying. Without it, you may get thrown out of the office.

Dan Weilbaker had that happen to him. He's now McKesson Professor of Sales at Northern Illinois University, but he began his working life as a pharmaceutical salesperson and became a national sales and marketing manager before entering academia. He recalls that very early in his career, he followed the company program conscientiously: Go into the doctor's office and say this and do that. Dan says, "I didn't care what the doctor's worries

97

were; I was going to tell him what I wanted to tell him." He certainly was not in the office to have a dialogue, meaningful or otherwise. He knew that doctors, like virtually all customers, are busy people; they don't have time for idle chitchat.

One day, Dan reached a doctor who'd had enough. "He told me, 'You don't care anything about what my concerns are. You are here to just push your product and I am not interested. Get out!' That was traumatic for a young salesperson. But it taught me I needed to be concerned more about their issues than mine."

When you set up the salesperson-buyer dynamic, you are already in trouble. If prospects are really guarded, it is going to be tough to get them to buy anything. If you can't get customers talking in general by creating the condition and the environment in which they feel safe and want to open up, then it is difficult to move on to learning about their situation. They will not volunteer any real information that will help you understand their challenges, needs, or wants when they're uncomfortable talking with you.

As discussed in Chapter 4, you want to keep the atmosphere as comfortable as possible for the prospect from the moment you walk into the office. The goal is to develop interest and initiate and maintain a real conversation—and again it is a sales conversation, not a sales call. Ask open-ended questions in a nonthreatening way, leaving the door open to a genuine answer. It doesn't always work, but that's the goal.

MEANINGFUL DIALOGUE CAN BE INVALUABLE

Even when the purpose of a meeting is not an immediate sale, it can be invaluable to have a meaningful dialogue with a customer because your relationship is so solid. Mike Accardi saw that when a good customer called him one night. Mike, who sells packaging systems and materials in Memphis, says that he had a very good customer for whom Wurzburg (Mike's company), maintained an inventory of 40 different box sizes. The customer used all sizes but didn't want to store them in his building. Mike would visit the customer twice a week and send what he needed the next day. Everything ran smoothly for 15 years, until the customer was caught in a political battle with an executive at his home office. The home office started making efforts to embarrass Mike's customer, and after five months found they could buy one of the 40 boxes in Kansas City and have it shipped to Memphis for less than Wurzburg was charging for the same box.

"My friend called me one night about 9:00," says Mike. "He was screaming and cussing. He said, 'I trusted you! You've been my friend all my life! I can't believe you screwed me.' I said, 'Hey, calm down. What's this all about?' He blurted out the story of this particular box. I said, 'Listen, I'm not going to talk to you right now. I'm certainly not going to listen to you cussing me out over my home phone. But I will be in your office tomorrow at 3:00.'"

The next day in the customer's office, Mike invited him to go down the street for a cup of coffee. He felt that if they stayed in the customer's office, they could not have the conversation Mike wanted to have; the phone would ring constantly and people would regularly interrupt. As Mike recalls, they went to the coffee shop, and over coffee he said to his friend, "Last night's call was very disturbing. And I don't mind telling you—number one I don't like to be cussed at, but after we hung up, I didn't sleep very much. I found myself thinking: have I done something to deserve that? Or have I overlooked something that I should have seen if I was going to be a true partner in your business? So I spent all last night going over the last 15 years in my mind as well as I could remember it about our relationship. I'm going to tell you something. Even if I'd known today was coming, I would not change one thing I've done, because for 15 years I've been your inventory manager and your purchasing agent. I am the only person in the building that you pay only when I perform. You don't buy any insurance on me; you don't pay any FICA on me, and you don't have anybody in the building who works harder for you than I do."

Mike says that when he stopped, the friend dropped his head and seemed almost on the point of tears. He looked up at Mike and said, "You just don't understand. My job is on the line, and they threw you in my face."

Mike asked the price of the competitive box and the customer told him. Even as a giant wholesaler, Wurzburg could not ordinarily buy the box for that price, let alone have it shipped to Memphis. The customer asked the logical question, "So how can they do it in Kansas City?"

Several years ago, says Mike, there were corrugated box factories all over the country and by the nature of the production process, once you turn the manufacturing plant on, you can never turn it off unless you shut it down and go out of business. At the time, Kansas City was unusual for a city its size because it had several corrugated box factories. The home office had found one plant that would run the box, probably to maintain production, and sell it for far less than Mike's price.

Mike said to his friend, "But look at this. Now we're going to talk about the cost of the box. In order for you to get that price, you have to take a forty-foot trailer into your building and you tie your money up for about six weeks. You are losing interest on that money. Plus you have tied up your space and your space is worth something. With me, you only pay for what you're using. You never have to worry about running out. What happens if you don't time the next truckload properly and you run out of this box? Kansas City is a two-day drive. What happens if they miss a day? How many dollars do you lose by not making shipment? That's the price of the packaging. It's not the cost of the box." The customer, at some level, of course, knew all this and agreed with Mike, but it made no difference. Mike lost the order and not long after, the customer lost his job.

When the customer found another job in Kentucky, however, and needed packaging, he gave the business to Mike. Indeed, the new account ordered enough that Wurzburg set up a branch to service the customer. But without a meaningful dialogue, Mike would never have known what hit him. Nor would he have been likely to get the business in Kentucky.

To engage customers in meaningful dialogue, keep the following six principles in mind:

1. Prepare for the call, not because it's important to you, but because it's important to them.

2. Focus on their issues and concerns, not yours.

3. Establish a safe environment by the words you use; your goal is to understand their situation, not necessarily to make a sale.

4. Encourage a dialogue; don't sound like the typical seller.

5. Remember all conversations are voluntary, and the ideal listen/talk ratio is 50/50.

6. Meaningful dialogue begins with intent and ends with your assessment.

Follow these six principles, and you can become a master of meaningful dialogue, sell more, and have much more fun.

PREPARE FOR THE CALL BECAUSE IT'S IMPORTANT

Preparation is paramount to having a meaningful dialogue. You must know as much as possible about the prospect's industry, business, situation before you walk into a meeting. You must want to get the other person interested in what you have to say. You do that by asking questions that encourage the person to want to learn more or share more openly. Remember that people only want to learn more if they believe you are objective and are not trying to put one over on them. Dialogue is elevated from just talking and listening to *meaningfulness* when our communications are credible. The way to indicate your objectivity is to ask serious questions about what matters most to the customer and by actively listening to the answers. The questions you ask will stimulate your customers to think differently, and by thinking differently, they will act differently. And the best way they can act differently is by buying your product or service when they conclude that it is in their best interest.

Note that making a purchase is different from selling. If a man visits a store to buy socks, that is a purchase, not a sale. He goes there to buy; nobody engages him or explains the features and benefits of different styles, colors, or sizes. A clerk might show him the display and add that there is a special on a particular sock this week—but that is still not selling, it is purchasing. The reason this is not a sale is that personal interaction was not necessary for money to change hands. The more complex the sale, the more meaningful the dialogue must be.

Salespeople ought to prepare for every sales conversation, not because it is important to them (although it is), but because it is important to the customer. Tim Wackel, a former sales executive who is now a sales consultant, speaker, and trainer and who heads The Wackel Group in Dallas, Texas, tells me that he will typically start a sales conversation by saying something like, "Hey, in preparing for our meeting today [or, in preparing for our phone call today], I spent some time. I Googled your web site. . . . I looked at your bio. . . . I looked at your last three quarterly reports." Tim wants customers to know that he has done his research and he plans to say something to provoke their curiosity and to show that he is interested in them.

"In my mind," says Tim, "the first decision they are going to make is whether this is an issue worth talking about. So the first part is making them curious, and then the second part—which happens very quickly thereafter; all this is happening real time in seconds, not in hours and days—is that I have to demonstrate my credibility. So the first decision is: Is this an issue worth talking about? Then the second decision is: Is this someone I want to talk to about this issue?"

Only if the prospect is both curious and regards Tim as credible and trustworthy can the sales conversation continue. Selling involves two people having a conversation, and the more meaningful the better. Reaching this point requires managing the steps in the customer/sales rep interaction. For people to act differently than in the past, they must think differently in the present and the future. To stimulate someone to think, a conversation must occur in which statements are so provocative, compassionate, or inflammatory that they require commentary. Or one of the parties might ask a question because of believing the other has some information that could be useful or interesting. If you cannot engage prospects or customers in a truthful conversation about their real issues, the likelihood you will change their behavior is very small. Without thoroughly understanding prospective customers' real issues, you waste their time and yours. And to avoid this, you must prepare for the conversation.

A client once called to ask for help in improving market share. As a market leader, the company had been losing share, it was bothersome to management, and they were unsure how to address it. Because the company had been the market leader, this was an unusual situation for them, so they asked us to meet with them.

The potential business was important to us, so we commissioned a $5,000 market research study before we went to the meeting. I had no idea whether we would get the project, but I knew we wouldn't get it if we were not prepared. I went to the meeting not only with questions but also with insights they didn't have. The research company had found and talked to 10 customers who had switched from the client's product to the competitor's and explained why.

At the meeting, we said, "This is how these people see your product, and this is how they see the competitive product."

They were blown away by the insight from our market research. Customers weren't hearing their message, so they realized they had a messaging problem. We created a meaningful dialogue because we came prepared with some original insights. Granted, it was a small sample, only 10 customers. And granted, it might not have represented what was happening in the marketplace generally. But here were 10 people who had switched from one product to another, and this is what they said. In some cases, our information simply confirmed the executives' own thinking, but it also told them they needed outside expertise to deal with a specific issue. That is where we brought value.

We created meaningful dialogue by doing research, by obtaining insights, and then by asking questions and sharing our insights. We did not share our insights as if they were the solution, but we used them to formulate questions that neither the company's managers nor we could answer. They were, however, questions that management needed to answer to tackle their problem, and they hired us to help them do just that.

FOCUS ON THEIR ISSUES AND CONCERNS, NOT YOURS

The best way I've found to encourage a meaningful dialogue is to focus on the other person. What does he care about? What does she like? What is he interested in? What does she like to do when she's not working? What would he like to do more of but does not have time to do?

There is no secret here. If you are genuinely curious about other people, ask them serious questions, and listen attentively to the answers, you can have a dialogue with most people (but not everyone; a few people are so stressed they cannot take a moment to consider even their own issues).

Henry Potts, the national sales manager for Melillo Consulting, says, "For the dialogue to be meaningful, it has to be about the customer. They know why I am there, and I know why I am there, and what we want to really get to is a relationship where we are sharing meaningful information. They may not know much about me, but that's not important in my first engagement with them."

In his first meeting, Henry typically does not spend much time talking about himself or his company, "though I will slide little bits in along the way." The real objective is to understand the customer. Henry focuses most of his questions on the specifics of the customer's business because that is what the dialogue is generally about. He tries to focus on the customer's business issues. What problems is the company routinely trying to solve? "That's what I want to get to, because that is where the nuggets are for me as a sales professional."

But ultimately, he says, "you need to get customers talking about themselves, their business issues, the challenges they experience in their daily activities. When I do that, I tend to get a meaningful dialogue. Or at least what happens is I get to recognize whether the dialogue is meaningful. Are they just giving me standard stuff? Or am I sensing that they are really giving me significant information?"

Traditional sales calls rarely create a comfortable atmosphere for the customer; therefore they do not usually promote meaningful dialogue. The average salesperson generally promotes passive listening by the customer/prospect—if that. When a prospect only listens passively, the salesperson is not likely to make a sale because the prospect is not engaged. If the salesperson performs a monologue—even a polished monologue—it is not likely to result in a sale. And if it does, that "sale" does not usually have great staying power. The odds of a sale are not very good if the salesperson cannot stir customers to think seriously about what is being suggested and respond in a way that enables the salesperson to answer the challenges to the premise that this product makes sense.

Sometimes even a dialogue can run into a cul-de-sac. The customer's responses are evasive or don't ring true. The prospect mouths a company line. You find you are talking around the subject rather than addressing it. What then?

Tim Wackel says, "I am at that stage in my life and my career where if the exchange is not honest, if it doesn't feel open, if it feels like there is something else going on, I'm going to ask about it. I am going to address it, but I am going to do so in a professional manner."

He will typically say something along the following lines: "Let me just kind of stop this right here. I have to apologize, because I really feel that I am not connecting with you. I feel that there is a tone in our conversation that is not productive for you and is not productive for me. First off, I would like to ask for your forgiveness, because I obviously have done something wrong, and then I would like to ask for your permission to learn where we have gone off-track. What have I said or done that caused this to go in a direction neither of us want it to go?"

Note that Tim takes all the blame for any miscommunication or misunderstanding, always a good tactic. He also points out that if the dialogue is not meaningful, it is not productive for the customer. While your time is often more precious than the customer's (if you're on commission and the customer is on salary, that's certainly true), your stated position is that you don't want to waste the customer's valuable time. Tim's experience is that "if you gently confront people with the truth—and confront is a strong word—but when you do that, you will be amazed—I am amazed—at what happens." The dialogue suddenly becomes meaningful in virtually every case.

ESTABLISH A SAFE ENVIRONMENT

Safe environments lead to success in selling in a big way. You establish a safe environment by the words you use. This point cannot be overemphasized. Your goal at this point is to learn, not to sell; to diagnose, not to prescribe. You want to understand the customer's situation, not necessarily make a sale. At the same time, you would like to provoke thought and open customers' minds to possibilities they may not have considered.

Sometimes it takes more than one call to establish a meaningful dialogue, but it never happens without preparation and thinking carefully about the words you plan to use. Few would be willing to argue that in selling, influencing, or persuading, words *don't* matter. Only when something is compelling is it likely to change behavior. To be compelling, words must combine the right amount of emotion with logic. It makes perfect sense; it is clear and logical. It can be proven by testimonials, by research, by experience, by a respected third party, or all four. It engenders thinking and movement to action. It paints a picture the listener is familiar with. It addresses a want, even one about which the listener may not yet be aware. (I'll be talking about ways to identify customer wants in Chapter 6.)

Because words and their order matter, consider how the words in essentially the same question can affect a situation differently. You can ask a prospect, "What associations are you involved with?" This is a perfectly reasonable question. But if the answer is "None," you've made the person uncomfortable, not the condition you want to create.

You want to know about the customer's participation in professional associations (the content), but you also want the person to feel positive after you've asked the question (the condition). A better question is, "What associations, if any, do you have the time to be involved with?" This permits the customer to say "None" without feeling inadequate.

Pharmaceutical salespeople often ask physicians, "How important is safety?" If the class of drugs is generally considered safe, doctors will say it's not important at all. In contrast, when salespeople ask, "Is safety important?" doctors will say it is important even about drugs that are considered safe. Likewise, it is the difference between asking, "How important is on-time delivery to you?" and asking, "Is on-time delivery important to you?"

What if you and a person with whom you have a good relationship are having a meaningful dialogue, and you happen to misspeak and say, "Is safety important?" The doctor is liable to say, "Yes safety is important, but this is a class of drugs that is considered very safe." You won't even have to ask the question properly. Because you're having a meaningful dialogue, the doctor will offer it up to you. Or, the purchasing agent will tell you, "Yes, delivery's important, but the reality is every company delivers 24/7."

When you're having meaningful dialogue, customers openly and willingly share the truth with you. They want to understand what you have to offer because you've telegraphed and signaled your pure intent—you really want to learn if there is a fit between what you are offering and their need. They are trying to help you find that fit, but if it's not there, they want to know that, too.

Because the words you use are so important, you should try to find the most compelling arrangement possible.

One of the greatest examples of compelling words begins: "Four score and seven years ago our fathers brought forth, upon this continent, a new nation, conceived in Liberty, and dedicated to the proposition that all men are created equal. Now we are engaged in a great civil war, testing whether that nation, or any nation, so conceived, and so dedicated, can long endure." Few of us, can write a Gettysburg Address. But we can learn to create powerful and persuasive sales messages by using the same compelling logic, emotion, and movement to action.

Once you are skilled at engendering meaningful dialogue effectively and consistently, you can engage people on a far more frequent basis and ultimately sell more.

Here is an apocryphal story Harry Mills tells in *Artful Persuasion* to suggest the power of saying something the right way: A Jesuit priest and a Benedictine monk were addicted chain smokers. They spent large portions of their day praying, all the while craving a cigarette. After talking about their problem, they agreed to discuss it with their superiors and report back.

When they met again, the Jesuit asked the Benedictine how his meeting had gone. "Disastrous! I asked the abbot, 'Will you give me permission to smoke while I'm praying?' and he was furious. He gave me fifteen extra penances as punishment for my irreverence. But you look happy, my brother, what happened to you?"

The Jesuit smiled. "I went to my rector and asked, 'May I have permission to pray while I'm smoking?' Not only did he give me permission, but he congratulated me on my piety."[1]

Because words matter, two heads are better than one. Share your words with someone you trust and learn from others. Ask for feedback: "Does that make sense to you? Does that sound right?" You should try to get that feedback in practice, from your colleagues, from your manager, from consultants. They can help you think about the best way to say something. What is the point you are trying to make and what is the best way to say it?

ENCOURAGE A DIALOGUE

I've said this about five different ways already, so I am not going to repeat it again.

ALL CONVERSATIONS ARE VOLUNTARY

Remember that all conversations are voluntary, so it is important to manage both the content and condition of the call. Great selling requires you to create dialogue throughout the sales interaction. A meaningful dialogue reflects your ability to foster an environment in which great conversations can occur between you and the customer/prospect.

In a meaningful dialogue, it is the salesperson's responsibility to pay attention and to manage the listen/talk ratio. You want to ensure that the prospect or customer talks at least 25 or 30 percent of the time during the ebb and flow of the interaction. It is hard to get two people in any conversation to share equally, especially when the agendas are different or the focus of the sales conversation isn't grounded in pure intent. If the customer is really interested, however, you can easily encourage a 70/30 or 60/40 listen/talk ratio. As the salesperson, you are usually advancing the hypothesis or the major concepts and doing most of the talking in some parts of the interaction, but you want—actually need—the other person to respond.

Salespeople traditionally approach selling by reinforcing the conditions in which prospects act like buyers, not like people who want to have a conversation. If you don't start by creating the condition where meaningful dialogue can prosper, it is unlikely you will end well because the other person will treat you like a typical salesperson. You cannot participate in a meaningful dialogue because the other person is guarded, defensive, and uncooperative—the opposite of what you want and need to be effective.

So the crucial question becomes, "How do you get people to *want* to listen to you?" First, you must convey to them that you want to understand their points of view and that nothing is more important than what they think. Next, ask questions and keep them real so customers desire to participate in a genuine discussion with you. The questions you ask must be crafted with the customers in mind and designed to obtain genuine, substantial, and honest feedback, without wasting the customer's (or your) time. You don't want your questions to send prospects running because you have signaled that you plan to sell them in the next breath. You should never appear insincere by asking questions designed to be a springboard for jumping into some product advantage you are pushing.

Some salespeople craft questions designed to provoke the answers they want: "If I could show you how to save $500 a month on your long distance service, would you be interested?" That is not the catalyst for meaningful dialogue. Be careful because this manipulative question is designed to trigger the answer the salesperson wants. Instead, you could ask something like, "Would you mind if I ask you a question? How important is price to you or your company when choosing a long distance provider?" This question does not set them up for a yes or no answer. It creates a safe environment for two reasons. First, you are asking permission to obtain information and second, you are inquiring about how important price is to them or their company, not setting them up for a pitch. This type of question will usually engender thinking and encourage meaningful dialogue. It will also give you information about the importance of price in their decision-making process.

MEANINGFUL DIALOGUE BEGINS WITH INTENT

Like everything else in the sales interaction, meaningful dialogue really begins with intent. The likelihood that you are going to have meaningful dialogue is driven more by your intent than almost anything else. Remember, if your purpose is to find out what people want and help them get it—to first diagnose then to prescribe—you are more likely to have meaningful dialogue than if your intent is to sell something *today*. Your intent will drive how you manage the condition and the content of the call.

With the proper intent—I am here to see if my company and product or service can be valuable to this prospect at this time—and extensive knowledge, I have no difficulty asking great questions because I no longer have to think about them. My conversations with prospects are like those I have with my best friends, and I don't use sales lingo that's designed to manipulate the customer into saying yes. Rather, I focus on what information I really need or would like to know: What can this person tell me that will help me learn whether our products or services make any sense in this situation?

During early sales calls with a prospect, I am more like an investigative reporter than a salesperson; and during the later calls I am much more like a consultant than a traditional salesperson. I am not there to sell something; rather, I am there to find out how (and if) my brand fits into their needs. I am there to understand how I can help them "see/believe" that my product or service will optimize their situation/results/outcomes based on what I learn about what they want. That does not exclude the occasional time where I have to go for broke and ask the hard question because all else has failed to resonate with the prospect/customer. I have nothing to lose. When those circumstances arise, I simply try to ask the hard question . . . softly.

An example might be something like this: "I realize that making a decision to change suppliers is a tough one. I really feel like we have done a lot to earn your business though it still seems we are far apart. In situations like this, the problem is usually that someone from our company got you upset (and maybe that was me); our sales message hasn't resonated with you; or you have a relationship with another supplier that is difficult to unwind. Is it okay if I ask if any of these are the case, and if so, what—if anything—would you suggest we might do to earn even a small piece of your business?"

MEANINGFUL DIALOGUE ENDS WITH YOUR ASSESSMENT

Finally, meaningful dialogue should end with your assessment of whether a successful exchange happened. Did you do the things suggested here, and was there meaningful dialogue? Did you provoke thinking? What was the listen/talk ratio? Did you manage the condition and create a safe environment so that the customer felt comfortable and willing to talk?

Anthony Yim found that a meaningful dialogue over time could overcome competitive challenges. Anthony's company received a call from a well-known consumer products manufacturer that was planning a new headquarters building designed by a famous architect. It was to be state-of-the-art, completely different from anything anyone had ever done. They wanted to be the paperless office of the future and have a cutting edge telecommunications phone system and network. Because it was a new building, the project was sizable—and the prospect was not then using Anthony's company (a telecom firm).

"A lot of people told me I should not waste my time with the account," he says. "They don't use us . . . it's hard to replace the other guy . . . the only reason they're inviting you in is because they need two or three bids . . . they just want to pick your brain. I thought, let me just try to see what we can do to build the relationship. They can listen to us, and hear our story."

Because it was early in the process, the prospect company's executives had decided, Anthony says, that even though they had a telecommunications supplier, they wanted to see what else might be available for the new building. Anthony participated in a number of brainstorming meetings with them: Let's put a cell tower outside the building and do cellular phones inside. Let's use a European standard. Let's do all kinds of whiz-bang innovations. Anthony met with them six or seven times to talk about all the ideas—most either impractical or impossible. "But I listened and established a meaningful dialogue. It never occurred to me to try to sell them on something, because we were in this process of brainstorming and I knew none of these ideas were ever going to come to fruition. They were just too off the wall."

Anthony brought people from his company into meetings and they validated that the prospect was trying to do something unique. "They set it up for when the customer finally got out of the fog, and realized some of the things they wanted were really a little pie in the sky. We went through the process, and my people kept saying to me, 'Well, you know, these guys are not the typical profile that buys from us; it's a long shot.' "

In the beginning, people warned Anthony that the prospect was just calling him in to pick his brains. He had to send any sale he made through a distributor who told him, "It's never going to happen. I know these guys. I'm in the territory; the other guys are going to kill us on price. And they're better positioned."

Because Anthony knew the dialogue with the customer was truthful, he could tell the distributor, "I don't think so. We've spent time and I don't think the other guys are better positioned; they're going to try to sell costs. They're going to rest on their laurels."

When the new headquarters building was starting to take shape, Anthony and engineers from his company walked around the site with the customer's representatives. "We asked, 'How would this work? How would that work?' It was showing interest and caring about their situation, and seeing how we would fit in. Because of that, we got a chance to tell our story and we eventually brought the customer up to our headquarters and then they really listened to the story. We went around our headquarters and showed them all the things we do, how we develop things. They were very receptive. They felt like this was home. They felt they were welcome, and they were there to listen. They could hear and see the solutions. They could see the benefit."

But a meaningful dialogue and all the steps along the way—Anthony met with the client more than a dozen times—was the setup so that when everyone became serious about discussing the details, their minds were open. "We had a meaningful dialogue," says Anthony. "And then we were allowed to tell our story."

Valerie Sokolosky at Valerie & Company in Dallas had a different experience, but her analysis of the dialogue taught her a valuable lesson.

An executive from a major nonprofit organization was looking for a professional presence program—how to be a professional in the workplace. It is a subject on which Valerie speaks and she has written several books on professional image and business etiquette. The prospect and Valerie communicated by phone and e-mail for a couple of months. The customer wanted a custom-produced hour presentation. She wanted Valerie's organization to take new pictures of tattoos, body piercing, and cropped pants that Valerie would weave into the carefully tailored presentation. The customer planned to also make a video recording of Valerie's presentation and put it in the organization's library so it would be a resource for employees in the future. (And, not incidentally, would not require Valerie to return for another presentation.)

"We had good conversations," says Valerie. "I sent her copies of my books, more than I normally send anybody. She went into the web site, and I'm sure she called other people." After two months, the prospective customer was finally ready to meet with Valerie. The meeting included the customer, the customer's boss, and the human relations director. They wanted Valerie's help in encouraging employees to dress properly. Valerie had brought her book, *Business Casual, Clarify Please,* and said, "This book is a quick, easy read. It's an inexpensive and valuable guideline that would be a good resource to give to everyone while I speak."

The customer rudely cut her off. "We're not carrying your book because it's called *Business Casual*. Here we use the words 'business appropriate.' "

Valerie had offended her and didn't know it. She responded, "Well, I can understand that, and I think you have great words in 'business appropriate,' but I also have to say (speaking with a smile and a light voice) I don't think you can find a book out there called *Business Appropriate*."

Looking back, says Valerie, "That seemed to destroy the rapport that had been built over several months. I didn't catch on to her body language and tone of voice when she cut me off. She was really saying, 'I am the boss. Listen to me.' She was in front of her boss, so she was giving a little muscle, if you will, to the vendor. I didn't pick up on that. Then she asked about price, and seemed surprised at the fee." Valerie was surprised at her surprise because the executive who had referred Valerie in the first place had indicated that her fee range would not be a problem.

The customer said nothing, the HR person said nothing, the boss said nothing. The meeting was over and Valerie returned to her office where she found an e-mail from the customer: "I have to look into other people. The price is not within our budget."

At that point, says Valerie, "I no longer had a relationship, a client, or a prospect." In assessing what went wrong and why there was no meaningful dialogue, Valerie realized she should have clarified at the very beginning of the process the organization's budget. "I made an assumption—don't ever make any assumptions—and the back-and-forth seemed to be flowing so easily that price never came up. It was totally my problem. I didn't address it up front, and then by the time I got to the meeting, when she said what she did about my book, I didn't read her. She turned out to be a young woman who was taken with the fact that her boss had let her find somebody and make the decision." By making an assumption that turned out to be erroneous, Valerie inhibited meaningful dialogue.

Meaningful dialogue can happen almost instantaneously or it can take time. There is no way to know whether it will happen quickly or over time. When I started my current business, one of the first calls I made included the VP of sales and marketing, the director of sales, and the director of marketing at a company planning to launch a new product. Having briefed myself on the company and its plans, I asked some questions they found difficult to answer. One was: What role does a relationship with prospects and customers play in the success and launch of this product? They said it had everything to do with the success.

I asked, "Have you taught your salespeople how to build relationships?" They said they had not. "What kind of relationships does your competitor have?" They said the competitor has great relationships. "What sales expert are you working with to help you prepare to compete against this competitor?" They said they were not working with anyone. I said, "You have a billion-dollar forecast and you are going to bet a billion dollars that the three of you can hire a sales force, get this product ready for launch, and at the same time make sure your sales force is prepared to beat your competition."

They were sufficiently provoked by the questions that they wanted me to meet privately with the director of sales, who would be the ultimate decision maker. I met with him at breakfast and we wound up spending three hours together. He later told me that when we first started, he was skeptical. During my initial presentation, he thought: Who is this guy to come in here and probe what we're doing? I sensed that he was skeptical and that we needed another meeting to have a meaningful dialogue in a one-on-one setting; I believed would be the only way I would get the business.

After our three-hour breakfast, he said, "Getting to know you better, I understand that we're not prepared at all." My assessment of needing to meet with him to understand his issues (not just the organization's issues), and to be sure that my interests were aligned with his created the opportunity to have a meaningful dialogue—and to do business. The assessment made the difference.

The questions we ask and the environment in which we ask them should engage customers' interest and encourage them to converse truthfully with us. Great salespeople have long known you simply cannot get to the top of a buyer's list until you get to the bottom of that buyer's beliefs. Preparing for and participating in more meaningful dialogue will elevate you in the customers' eyes and be a key to your success. Only after you have created a safe environment and the meaningful dialogue begins will you get the details you need to understand the prospective customer's situation/problem/challenge.

CHAPTER 6

LEARN THE SITUATION, PROBLEM, OR CHALLENGE

The best way to begin to learn the situation is by doing your homework before you meet prospects or customers. While it is not the only way, you need a connection or some knowledge of their business on which to launch a discussion and understanding of the specifics of their situation.

We need to uncover exactly what prospective customers want or need. Is it clear to them? Is it serious enough—or important enough—that they are willing to do something about it? Once you have begun a meaningful dialogue and there is a real two-way conversation, you can begin to learn the situation/problem/challenge, which is the next step in the DELTA process. The best way to do that is by the questions you ask.

Salespeople have been trained for years to ask qualifying questions. "What are the problems that keep you up a night?" "About how many shipments do you make a month?" "Are you satisfied with the productivity of your metal-cutting machines?" You want to be careful, however, in the way you probe to understand a prospect's challenges. When Sean Feeney was a vice president of sales (he is now CEO and president of Inovis, an Atlanta-based software company), he once asked a senior executive, "What are the issues you are struggling with?"

The executive bristled. "You know, Sean, you sales guys are all reading the same book. You all come in, you all want me to tell you all my problems. If I spent my time educating all you guys on my problems, I'd never get any work done. I expect you to come to me with an understanding of what my problems are and tell me what the solutions are."

It helps, therefore, if you already understand in general what a prospect's situation/problem/challenge is likely to be. Tim Wackel at The Wackel Group says, "When I am trying to develop new clients who are sales executives, I try to figure out what their pains are. I may or may not be able to get specific information, but I can probably venture some pretty good guesses. Having been a sales executive myself, there are some common ills that most sales executives are still experiencing. If I can connect by making them curious it's a start: Is this a problem you're having within your organization? Because if it is, we have some proven ideas that have really driven some tremendous results, and we would love to have the opportunity to talk to you about them."

If it is true that selling greatness usually occurs when we can get customers to want to converse with us, then we must either say something incredibly compelling, interesting, unexpected, or surprising—or ask great questions. Most people have a fairly short attention span, so they are not likely to listen very long unless we somehow engage them. Canned sales stories are rarely compelling in the customer's mind, whereas good questions can grasp and hold a prospect's interest. Get most people talking about themselves, their business, their problems, and their challenges and you probably have their attention. And once you have that, it helps to know a prospective customer's typical situation well enough to know where there is liable to be pain.

Use the meaningful dialogue you've created to ask questions that get you to a point where you truly understand whether there's a fit between what the prospect wants and what you can offer. In a sales conversation, questions do at least three things:

1. Good questions force people to think.
2. Good questions promote dialogue.
3. Good questions obtain information.

Bad questions either make people uncomfortable or attempt to force an answer the salesperson wants. Often salespeople ask questions designed primarily to elicit a response that becomes a launchpad for their story. In the "stimulus-response strategy," the salesperson asks a series of positive leading questions such as, "If I could show you how to save $5,000 a month on your delivery costs, would you be interested?" Who could say no? Indeed, the customer is supposed to develop a habit of saying "yes" that leads to a positive response to the closing question. Unfortunately, it also appears to be manipulative and off-putting to sophisticated prospects—and these days prospects are more sophisticated than ever.

Before your first meeting make a comprehensive list of the questions you need answered to determine whether this customer is a fit for your product or service. Your questions ought to be built around your knowledge of the customer, the marketplace, your unassailable positions, and your competitor's unassailable positions. I spend an hour (and often two) before I go to meet somebody creating the questions I need answered to determine if a prospective client is a fit for what we offer. You have to create your own diagnostic tool, which is your own set of questions. Far too often, salespeople wing it.

So let's consider in more detail the three elements that define good questions.

GOOD QUESTIONS FORCE PEOPLE TO THINK

Ideally, you want to ask questions that force people to think. Mental self-inquiry is a powerful tool in selling and persuading. You don't have to think very deeply when somebody asks, "Where are you from?" But you might need to think for a while if somebody asks, "How do you feel about raising the age limit for Social Security?"

Good questions create the opportunity for you to learn how your customers and prospects think, and the questions give them an opportunity to formulate their thoughts (which in itself is powerful). Many times we ask questions about something people have not thought about before, or they haven't thought about it in the way we've framed the question. Often the real power of our questions is in helping people see or think of things differently.

Professor Dan Weilbaker of Northern Illinois University says that students in the sales program (like entry-level salespeople generally) tend to assume they know what is important to the customer. Or they assume they know what prospects are looking for and what they need without engaging them in a conversation or asking questions. "It's the old 'book and the cover' proverb: You think you know the book because you looked at the cover. For a beginning salesperson or student, this is one of the biggest obstacles we have to overcome. Because they have the product knowledge, they assume they can sell the product because they know what is important. I think knowledge itself is sometimes a culprit."

Everyone agrees that product knowledge is necessary, says Dan; it's the price of entry. But it becomes the culprit in hobbling sales performance because it tends to drive behavior. Salespeople sometimes feel that because they have the product knowledge, they know what is important and the customer doesn't.

Dan remembers a story about IBM: "When IBM was selling a lot of hardware, new salespeople would grow their business for about 20 months, and then business would suddenly plateau. Management tried to figure out what it was and finally learned that the salespeople, by the end of 20 months, had so much product knowledge and other information they could walk into an account and immediately tell the customer what would solve their problems."

But they couldn't sell the customer, because they were not even trying to learn the customer's situation. It was as if they did not involve the customer at all in the solution; because they knew so much, they were the resident experts. They could diagnose a problem quickly, but they didn't engage the customers. They didn't spend time building relationships or giving the customer a chance to talk so their sales hit a plateau.

That is the danger of focusing entirely on product knowledge. It gives salespeople the wrong idea of its importance; they then put product knowledge above everything else. They think they can ignore their mind-set and the business relationship because product knowledge is so important, it will do the entire job. But we know that it is not the case.

When you are setting up the questions that you intend to ask in a sales conversation, you want to use triggers and transparent motives to get customers to open up. Triggers are phrases that get the customer interested because they make reference to something that "triggered" your asking the question. Examples would be, "Last week I read an article that made me think that you might have a problem with . . ." "I was talking to John yesterday, and he told me . . ." "I went to the Natural History Museum last week and it made me think . . ." "I saw something online and it made me wonder do you ever . . . ?" Any event that provoked your observation and suggested a question for the customer is a trigger. A well-worded trigger creates interest and makes someone want to listen to the rest of your question and then answer it truthfully.

Transparent motives are also effective when setting up a question. The idea is to be transparent about your motives to yourself and to your customer. If you are open about your motives, it may change your behavior. How many salespeople would begin a call by announcing: "Good morning, Ms. Prospect. I'm here to sell you something today because I have to make this month's quota"? In contrast, a transparent motive like "I'm here to learn if there's a fit between what we offer and your situation" can be both true and engaging.

Focus on three key concepts when you are developing or crafting great questions:

1. *Intent:* Why am I asking this question? The answer should almost always be to learn something or uncover something that will help you see (and the customer discover) that there might be a fit between your product and the cus-

tomer's wants. The goal in asking questions is to deepen understanding on both sides. It's all about understanding.

2. *Content:* What exactly do I need to know? Usually you need facts or a deeper understanding of relative importance/urgency or both. Very straightforward.

3. *Condition:* The ultimate goal in a sales conversation is an exchange of the truth. The best way to have customers be truthful with us is to be truthful with them and to create low-pressure situations where customers feel safe telling us what we want to know. You accomplish this best by being ever mindful of the condition of the call. The words we use create the environment of the call, and if we ask questions in the right way, people are more likely to want to be truthful with us. As you are developing your questions, always consider how you can ask them in a nonthreatening and safe way.

In the financial services industry, a question like, "Does your business need a good return on its liquid funds?" is one virtually everyone will answer, "Yes"; but it focuses on price, which may not be ideal unless you can be sure of always offering the best return. A question like, "How important is it that you have instant access to all your deposits?" is more thought-provoking—and focuses on service.

In the pharmaceutical industry, a sales rep may ask doctors, "What do you want when you prescribe a drug?" Most will say they want one that works. Well . . . all drugs work to one degree or another. That answer does not tell you much. If you ask, however, "Is it fair to say that what you really want is a drug with the greatest likelihood for success?" they will say, "Yes, that's what I want." That is different from a drug that works, but most doctors haven't thought of drugs exactly that way before that moment.

GOOD QUESTIONS PROMOTE DIALOGUE

As pointed out in Chapter 5, a meaningful dialogue is an adult discussion of the truth or a free flow of meaning; it is a conversation, a back-and-forth. It is a dialogue that leads you to the right path to success. (Success, by the way, could be to learn that this person is not a good fit for you. Success could be to learn the next thing to do to move the sales process forward. Success is not always an order.) Good questions promote a dialogue when they are open-ended—they cannot be answered with a simple "Yes" or "No"—and do not carry an insidious assumption. The question, "Do you still beat your wife?" is close-ended, *and* it contains a malicious assumption: you beat your wife. It is a perfect example of a bad question.

In contrast, "What do you do when you're not working?" "Where did you go to school, and how did you choose it?" or "What is the most frustrating thing about being in your business today?" are open-ended. While they carry assumptions (the person does something when not working, went to school, has work-related frustrations), they are inoffensive. These questions are likely to promote a dialogue because they invite people to talk about things that are important to them.

Melvin Boaz says that if the salesperson has to ask what a prospect's problem is, "you probably don't know what your product can do for them." Melvin is a national sales manager for Smith & Nephew, an international orthopedic implant company, and he sells a computerized system for putting in artificial hips. He says, "You need to understand the value proposition of the product or service you're offering. It generally boils down to a relatively small group of solutions that your offering has, and you know from other customers that it does well in solving those problems. So, the question becomes, 'Do you ever . . . ?' Or, 'Have you experienced . . . ?' Or, 'Do you currently experience . . . ?' If customers say, 'That's exactly one of the issues that I have,' then you have a meaningful dialogue going on right away."

Sometimes prospective customers are not aware they even have the problem, says Melvin. So sometimes sales representatives must help quantify that the prospects *do* have a problem and what it means in their organization by asking questions that engender thinking. In business-to-business selling, answering the problem means saving money, making money, or both. Again, salespeople need to spend time understanding the account or the client for each sales call, making sure they know exactly what their offering is going to do for that client, and be able to quantify for the customer.

Melvin is currently selling a computer-assisted surgery device for joint implants. It helps navigate the incision, the placement, and the sizing of the implant to get better medical outcomes. His sales challenge is that surgeons will sometimes say that they think they already do a fine job. "And quite frankly, they do a fine job," says Melvin. He says the question should be whether the surgeons think there is room for improvement in what they are doing. "You have to find a way to tactfully get to that point with a surgeon, recognizing that surgeons have a high degree of confidence. To question their procedure capabilities is a delicate area, but at the same time it is not that difficult to have a conversation by asking if they think that things could be better." Here the question promotes a meaningful dialogue about the product and why they might want to consider making a change from what they are doing.

Often prospects do not think they have a problem at all, which is why salespeople have to do a certain amount of educating on every sales call without making it seem like criticizing or lecturing. In Melvin's situation, he says, "You have to be very tactful in your approach and, again, this is where you use other surgeons. You say, 'Dr. So-and-So, this was his experience. This is what he has experienced and this is what he says today. Would you be interested in something like that if you thought there would be a similar outcome?' That's the kind of discussion that might engage a surgeon."

There may be times when the information you learn doesn't lead you to another question or an opportunity to tell your story but it does lead you to an action that helps move the customer forward toward a purchase. For example, Sean Feeney learned from one customer that he needed to spend time in the field before he could answer whether there was a fit between what Sean's company offered and the customer's situation.

Sean had called on an executive who had recently been promoted to vice president of sales. When he met with the executive to talk about sales management software, Feeney said in effect, "Here are the other companies we work with. Here's what we have found their issues to be. Are these similar to your issues?"

The prospect said, "Well, we have some of those, Feeney, but I would really like to understand what you all can do, and you're going to have to figure out what that is, because I don't have time to teach you."

Sean said, "Let me go out and work with your top reps and talk to them about what's going on in the field, and what they need help with and then I'll come back and tell you what we can do." Sean, with the prospect's assistance and at his company's expense, spent time with three of the prospect's top reps around the country. When Sean came back, he said to the prospect, "Here is what I saw . . . here is what I found . . . here is where I think people make mistakes . . . and here is what I think we can do."

Over a five-month period, armed with the information he'd gathered in the field, Sean built a good relationship with the sales executive and his team. "We kept saying, 'Well, we will go out and field-prove this. We will go out and talk to your guys in the field, rather than just telling them what we're doing.' Ultimately we got that deal. And what I learned was bringing value beyond just selling them something, whether it is the consultative sell, or the solution sell, or the relationship. It is bringing value as an advisor as well as a solution-provider."

Sean adds, "The difficult part of relationship selling is often getting that initial 'in' to building that relationship. For that, you have to bring some credibility. You have to bring some nugget of value or empathy to their issue, and then show customers a way they can solve it."

There are several issues here. A prospect may not realize there is—or the extent of—a problem. Sometimes, prospects know there is a problem but don't know there is a solution. Often, prospects don't know what they want because they don't know what's available. And sometimes they think they know what

135

they want, but that's not the best solution. It's the salesperson's job to uncover what the prospect truly wants (or needs) and suggest the best option, and this is almost always best done with questions, not statements.

If you ask prospects what they want, they will usually respond, but most are not aware of all possible options. So, you must be sure the customer understands your proposition—your hypothesis—and how it compares with alternatives. The salesperson's responsibility is to help prospects and customers define what they really want, which may not be what they thought they wanted at the beginning of the sales process. Salespeople often assume they know what customers want (or would want if they only understood the product clearly), and the answer is their product.

You may identify situations, problems, or challenges that prospects say they want to solve, but in truth they don't want to solve them. Or, if they do, they don't want to solve them now. (Maybe later; they are way down on a list of priorities.) Part of what salespeople have to learn as they go through this process is whether this difficulty (or opportunity) seems important enough to the buyer to act now. And if not now, when?

Marketing professors Philip Kotler and Kevin Lane Keller point out that customers tend to have five types of needs. There are stated needs (the customer wants an inexpensive car); real needs (the customer wants a car whose operating cost, not its initial price, is low); unstated needs (the customer expects good service from the dealer); delight needs (the customer would like the dealer to include an onboard navigation system); and secret needs (the customer wants to be seen by friends as a savvy consumer).[1] The more needs and wants a salesperson can uncover with questions and then address them, the easier it is for the customer to buy.

Purchasing agents may say they want the lowest price when they really want on-time delivery or 99.9996 percent reliability. Price is always a consideration, but it is often necessary to put price into a context. Physicians often say they want a drug that is efficacious, but what they really want is a drug that has the greatest likelihood of success. The salesperson's job is to help prospects understand their alternatives and then have a planned conversation with them about the product and how it fits into their current need, or unrecognized want, or both. Interestingly, once the customer recognizes a want and its ramifications, it is often one your product answers. That becomes the "aha!" moment salespeople seek when they not only make the sale but are now trusted, valued, and the customer desires a professional relationship.

You may have heard the term "need-based selling." Do not confuse that concept with the ideas I'm advancing here. A need-based system teaches salespeople to identify (with questions) prospect or customer needs with the goal of selling products and services to satisfy a particular need.

Selling is actually based on wants. An individual needs food, water, clothing, and shelter. A business needs an offering, customers, and cash flow. The way individuals and businesses satisfy their needs is through wants, which are more specific. We may need food, but want a steak or a salad or sushi or baked beans or a candy bar. A business may need to ship documents around the country but want to use FedEx or the U.S. Postal Service or fax machines or e-mail. If a business has no need for a product or service, it is not a prospect, but establishing a need is only a beginning.

The problem is that too many organizations and people have wants (indeed, wants are almost unlimited), but don't want to solve them. Or at least not now. If you don't understand that selling is about wants, you are not going to ask the right questions to uncover them. You can identify needs, but if the need doesn't lead to a significant want, nothing happens.

You will be most effective when you help customers identify what they want right now as opposed to what they might need or be willing to buy some time in the future. Too often, salespeople will get prospects to identify a need and spend countless hours trying to convince them that their product or service can fill that need, yet no sale ever occurs. Why? Because the need may be real, but there is no requirement to solve it now.

Sean Feeney, speaking as a chief executive officer, says that frequently a salesperson can show a prospect a good return on investment (ROI), but is dealing with a person at the level where that problem isn't real to them; they don't feel the pain. "You also have to understand where the problem or need fits within the priority of the person you are calling on, his boss, that person's boss, and ultimately to the company. Sometimes I get shown things and I would love to do them. I can see, for example, how putting in a new financial management system would really help us. But it is not in the top five priorities, and so you can be the best salesperson in the world, and it is not going to make any difference. That is something we have slated for late 2007 or 2008, so go away until then."

A salesperson may make a watertight case for the new system, or the new milling machine, or the new mail-handling center, but it will make no difference. Sean says, "I think you have to understand where the purchase falls in the priorities, and where it falls in the pain meter within the group or the division or the corporation you are calling on. An individual employee or middle manager might have a lot of pain, but might not have the budget or the clout to solve it. From a corporation point of view, and from a budget point of view, I can say, 'Here is when we are going to fix it but we can get by on that until then.' So I think it is understanding what you are selling." The only way to get to that point is by asking questions.

If the sale is a $1,000 solution to a drippy restroom faucet in the restroom, that is pretty easy: let me show you how I am going to save you $5,000 over the year. If the sale is $4 million and is going to consume the organization for 16 months, that's much more difficult. "The easiest people to sell," says Sean, "are the people who understand what they are trying to do, and who know what it will look like when they have success. The biggest sales challenges are when the companies know they have pain, they really don't know what the solution looks like, and they are hoping that you are going to bring them magic. Those are the tough ones to sell to. The easy ones, where the ROI really works, is where they understand they have a problem, they understand what the solution looks like, and they have the business savvy to say, 'You know what? I understand that if I spend a million dollars now I am going to save five million dollars over the next three years. That is a big enough issue that we are going to take that one.'"

GOOD QUESTIONS CAN OBTAIN INFORMATION

You have to get a certain amount of information from the customer to determine whether there is a fit. The question is, what information and how do you get it? I said earlier that you have to create a comprehensive list, but getting the information is not just a function of knowing exactly what information you need. It is making sure that you ask the questions in a way that people want to answer them. If they don't want to answer them, they may give you facts and figures, but they won't give you the information you need to hold a useful sales conversation.

You can use questions to find out where somebody is from and how long they have lived in the area, to learn their business concerns and challenges, and to discover what is important to them. A large part of the value of the questions is not only the information you gain, but also the mental state the questions stimulate. Questions, if asked properly, can generate a feeling of caring and genuine interest on the other person's part as well as create the impression that you are insightful.

Asking a good question is an art, but you can promote useful answers in two ways: first, by creating an atmosphere of comfort and safety when you are with the other person (the condition of the call), and second, by the quality of your questions to further facilitate that safe feeling so the other person wants to answer truthfully and candidly.

The only way I've found to have a genuine relationship is to be honest and open, to be truly curious in the questions I ask, and to share information (but, again, not gossip). This may sound warm and fuzzy, yet not very practical. Does it do anything for the bottom line? Will it help a consultant or an accountant bring in more business? Will it help salespeople sell more? In fact, it will.

If people trust your word and trust your intentions because you are honest, open, and willing to share, they will be willing to work with you, to buy from you, to take your ideas into account. But to build that trust, you need to make sure that the people you ask actually want to answer the questions. Not that they always will. You may meet someone on a bad day who is too distracted to focus on you, and a few people will not be responsive no matter how you set up a question.

Usually you have to give information to get any. If you treat a sales call as an interrogation or as if you are filling out a marketing survey, you will quickly shut down the flow of information. The other person's degree of openness often reflects your own. If you won't tell other people what you do when you're not working, or where you went to college, or where you grew up, why should they tell you? Most people will show you their cards if you show yours. But it has to be a roughly equivalent exchange.

Linda Mullen, who sells Doncaster clothing directly to her clients, questions both the women her customers refer to her and the women she calls cold. Typically a referral is someone "qualified" to buy the clothes; she knows from Linda's customer what the clothes cost, the styles, and the quality. When Linda phones a prospect she does not know at all, she begins by saying something like, "Hi, we haven't had the pleasure of meeting, but I wanted to see if you would be interested in the service that I provide. I work with busy executive women, and I do trunk shows out of my home, and the reason I'm calling is to see if this is a service that might work for you."

If the prospect responds positively and asks for more information, Linda will begin to learn her situation: "Let me ask you a couple of questions. Do you like to go shopping?" And most say, "Oh my God, no!" Linda says that the service she provides and the clothing she represents are for the woman who has no time in her life. She tells prospects, "Women come to my home and meet with me, and spend about an hour, but they really appreciate the service and the advice that comes with it. Would you like to come in and take a peek to see if this is a service that works for you?" If the prospect says she's interested, Linda learns more: "Where do you typically go shopping? Is there a label you go for?"

Linda tells me, "I know all the labels, so if she drops a label that's lower than my ballpark price—and my average suit is $500 and then goes up from there—I know she may be uncomfortable with the prices. So if she says to me, 'Well, I go to Casual Corner,' my comeback is 'This is more than Casual Corner.' I give them another line so that they know what to expect: 'It's almost like Ann Taylor or Jones of New York. Would you consider spending more?' I have women say, 'No, I'm really comfortable with going to Casual Corner.' But I also have had women say, 'Well, you know I go there, and I never find what I'm looking for. So, yes, I would consider spending more.'"

When customers visit Linda for the first time, she learns as much as she can about their situation and need for clothes: "Tell me what you do. Who do you report to? Who reports to you? How much traveling do you do? How many black tie affairs do you go to in a season?" And the core question, "What is your biggest frustration when you go shopping?"

Recently, Linda met with a woman who was head of an $800 million company. She usually bought her clothes at Talbot's, which Linda sees as relatively low end compared with what she sells. "But she had been referred to me by two women in her company who already work with me, and she had been hearing about me and seeing their clothes, and so finally decided to come in. On the phone, I sensed her becoming really uncomfortable with the prices. But when she came in, she said, 'I tend to buy things on sale, and then I never have something to match it up with.' I suggested doing the fitting at the woman's house. I would do a closet audit with her, and help her weed out pieces she didn't wear or need any more. I could show her how to maximize what she already owned."

Linda did go to the woman's house, helped her clean out her closet, reorganized it, brought the new pieces in, and showed her how to mix and match the new with the old. "In the long run now, she has realized that she is spending her money more wisely. Although a Doncaster suit, say, may cost more than a suit on sale, it is actually less expensive per wearing because she is able to wear it so many more times. Some things she bought on sale she might be able to wear once and end up hanging in her closet. Her price per wearing with me went down in a huge way, and that is a large learning curve for some of my customers."

If you closely analyze Linda's approach, you will see she acquires a lot of information in the course of what appears to be—and I am certain sounds like—a normal conversation. She does not seem to be screening the women or performing an interrogation. Good questions obtain information without becoming a cross-examination. They do that by encouraging the person to answer truthfully so that the information is valuable. It enables you to extend the conversation and continue down the buying process if indeed there is a fit. Linda, in a conversational manner, was able to acquire lots of information that helped her move prospects along the buying continuum.

If you preface a question correctly, most people will answer it most of the time (but not always; again, this does not work all the time). Before you ask a question that might be sensitive or unexpected, think how you might preface it so it does not sound preemptory or intrusive.

All good questions seek truthful, honest, candid answers. But they often must be introduced in such a way that the other person actually responds with truthful, candid answers. So the way we ask, the language we choose, the way we introduce the question can dramatically affect the quality of the response. We should use the same rigor to plan our questions that we use to plan an important sales call, our performance appraisal, or our meeting with the boss.

You don't walk into a meeting and ask a customer you've never met, "What things would you want to do more of, but don't have time for?" It is a perfectly good question and can give you important insights into the customer's character, personality, and interests, but it has to be buffered. If you ask, "What do you do when you are not working?" and the person says, "I'm always working," you have an opportunity to say something like, "I know that feeling and I've always wondered what I would do if I had time to do it. Have you ever thought about what things you would like to do, but don't have time for?" Virtually everybody will answer the question if you set it up that way.

I suspect that people who are uncomfortable asking questions of a personal nature are uncomfortable sharing personal information. They have cognitive dissonance. They do not want to ask where someone goes on vacation because they do not want to be asked where they go on vacation. They do not want to ask what someone does when not working, because they do not want to be asked.

Nevertheless, such questions can help you build a positive relationship with prospects and customers while learning about their situation. Remember the difference between average salespeople and exceptional salespeople is in their mind-set, their messaging, and their ability to build valuable business relationships (ways to build a relationship are described in Chapter 9).

The quality of your questions is directly related to the quality of your business, because unless people change the way they think, they are not likely to change the way they act. If your objective is to have them do something different from what they currently do—the goal of almost all selling—the only sure way to do so is to change their thinking. You must not only provoke thought; you must have them think differently about the subject. The best way to do that is usually with questions and not statements.

Far too often, salespeople think they should ask questions to get information that uncovers customer wants and needs. What they really require is information that helps customers uncover their wants for themselves. This is an important distinction. You want the customer to say, "I never thought of it that way before." Then they will have identified a want they didn't realize they had.

If you have established your unassailable position (which I'll talk about in Chapter 7), you are ready to begin crafting questions that determine how customers value that position. If your unassailable position is that your company is the only one that can deliver in 24 hours, you have to ask about delivery. But you don't ask, "Is rapid delivery important to you?" Almost everyone will say it is. Instead, ask something like, "What percentage of the time is it absolutely, unequivocally necessary to get the product delivered in 24 hours?" If the answer is, "About half the time," you have earned the right to ask for half the business.

If the answer is, "Almost never, we don't run that way," then talking about how your firm can deliver in 24 hours is not going to persuade this prospect to change buying behavior. That does not mean delivery time is unimportant and you can't use it as a differentiator, because you can. But it does mean that if you are hanging your hat on rapid delivery, this prospect probably does not care.

You must also be aware that bad questions can create large obstructions and damage your credibility. We recently asked a rep how she approaches prospects. She said she asks, "Given the fact that our software has seven exclusive features, is used throughout the world, and is less expensive than our competitor's, is there any reason why you wouldn't use our software in the future?" How would you answer that question if you were the prospect? If you say, "Yes," you invite an argument. If you said, "No," you might not mean it and would just be saying it to pacify the rep.

More to the point, her question suggests that there is no reason a prospect would not buy her software, and it is difficult and unfair for her to ask prospects to be open-minded when her mind is obviously closed.

In selling, you are asking people to open their minds. When customers or prospects perceive that yours is closed, why would they open theirs? The kinds of questions you ask and the way you ask them says a lot about whether your mind is open or closed, whether you truly want to hear what the other person has to say. Thus, you want to avoid obvious leading questions that are difficult for the customer to answer or questions that sound like an interrogation.

Use the following advice to create questions that will set you apart and enable the prospect to view you as a resource.

Take the time to write your questions before you meet with the client, and use your questions to seek information to see if your product is a fit. Make certain that your questions explore and probe hot topics that are driving individual and company behavior. Word your questions in a way that identifies the thought process behind decision making. Finally, ask questions that seek information about the importance of the unassailable facts (features and benefits) of your product.

Questions are more influential than statements. In fact, they are the most powerful tool salespeople (and teachers) use. In our definition of selling—selling is educating—asking questions is the most effective way to help people learn things they didn't know or realize before. What you're really trying to do by asking these questions is to have customers conclude that your product or service fits their needs. The questions are designed to engender mental self-inquiry where the customer learns you are a fit.

The quality of your questions in selling determines the quality of your business. You need to engage customers in dialogue because if you cannot learn whether there is a fit between their wants and your product or service and you cannot provoke thought, it is unlikely you will do much business. The best way to make someone think, promote a dialogue, and obtain the information you need to see if there is a fit, is to ask open-ended, nonjudgmental questions that prospects are comfortable answering.

Once you know that there is a fit, it's time to tell your story.

CHAPTER 7

TELL YOUR STORY

We find it interesting that although many people in sales, while they often detest company-provided scripts, they often create their own scripts without realizing they're scripts. They just don't like the scripts the company gives them. They don't like the canned verbiage, which is fine—as long as they have something better to use and say. Usually, it's not, so the point of this chapter is to suggest ways you can improve even a very good script.

Every product or service needs effective positioning in the minds of customers and prospects. In today's marketplace, most sales experts agree few customers find traditional sales communication in the form of "features and benefits" to be highly persuasive. We also know that few salespeople, when asked to stand up and tell their product story—including compelling reasons why customers should use their product—do it well on a consistent basis. Or perhaps they have a canned speech, which frequently is less than optimal. We therefore encourage salespeople to develop their own story with great care and thought.

By *story,* I mean *cascading logic* in such a way that it connects with clients, who then understand how you and your product are truly different and are a fit for their situation. Based on the meaningful dialogue and questions you've asked, you now honestly believe there is a fit. Your clients sense it is a fit, and now it's time for you to connect the dots. Based on what they told you, you believe that your product or service is a fit for their situation or problems, and here's why.

The story needs to be compelling, logical, and visual. It should include analogies, anecdotes, or testimonials to which customers can relate easily. Ideally, they will see themselves in the story. You need to state a rationale for your story that specifically explains why you are advancing this idea. It needs to illuminate exactly why your product or service is a perfect fit in this situation. And lastly, it needs to tie back to the things you have learned in previous interactions with the customer about his (or her) individual business situation (in the Engage and Learn phases).

Every product or service probably has three or four stories, any one of which you should be able to tell extremely well because what is appropriate for one prospect may not be appropriate for another. If you develop only one story, you may be missing the sales to those customers who would respond to another story more appropriate to their wants. To do this, you must first understand what stories you can tell. For every product or service, there are several reasons somebody should buy and use it, and you must learn to tell those stories with great clarity and power.

So what are the six principles you can use to develop a powerful story?

1. Your story should be based on your unassailable positions and should be about positioning, not about competing with another company.

2. Your story should combine facts, features, benefits, questions, and anecdotes, but it needs to be clear, solid, repeatable, and powerful.

3. Your story needs to contain both logic and emotion.

4. Your story needs to be based on a premise or hypothesis that involves satisfying a customer want.

5. Your story must help customers see there is minimal risk in doing business with you.

6. Your story needs to be true.

In the rest of this chapter, I talk about each of these principles in detail.

BASE YOUR STORY ON AN UNASSAILABLE POSITIONING

From a sales perspective, unassailable positioning means that the merit of your product or service, if positioned in the market correctly, is undeniable. You have an unassailable position when a feature or benefit of your product exactly matches a customer need at an affordable price. Unassailable positioning is most important when your relationship with a prospect is not that solid. If the customer or prospect has a great relationship with another company, then your case has to be a lot stronger than the competitor's. Not only do buyers have to make the decision to buy from you, they have to defend that decision to their friend who is the competition.

One of the best examples of establishing an unassailable position is Southwest Airlines, the most financially successful airline flying today. They have established their position as the premier, low-cost, no-frills airline. You cannot dispute it, it is brilliant, and it works.

As an individual salesperson, how do you establish an unassailable position? You begin by having an in-depth understanding of your customers and what is important to them. You also need to understand every detail of your product and each of its potential advantages, both tangible and intangible. Regardless of the customer base, there is likely a place for your product or service that makes sense for most prospective (or qualified) customers if you present it clearly and position it well. That is the business you should own.

Let's further define what I mean. First, consider the unassailable truths about your product or service and clearly identify the position of each one. You do this by making a list of every undeniable truth about your product or service. Next, think about your customers' wants. Wednesday delivery might fit one customer. Low price might fit another. A third might want custom sizes and does not care (within reason) when they are delivered. For that customer, a custom size that you can always deliver when you promise at an acceptable price would be unassailable positioning. Finally, have great clarity about the places where the use of your product is incredibly difficult, if not impossible, to debate and aligns with a customer want.

Mike Accardi, selling packaging in Memphis, makes an interesting point: "In all my career, I have looked to see if there was any way we could come up with an exclusive. This would be the only place you could buy this product and you had to buy it from me. That would be like clipping coupons. It has taken me my whole career to find that exclusive, and now I have it. I don't sell tape or stretch wrap or boxes or strapping or labels. Those are all products my customers can buy from any number of vendors. When I go into a customer, I sell the only exclusive I have—and that's me. For my customers to get me, they have to buy their packaging products from Wurzburg." A top salesperson is an intangible benefit that adds value to any offering.

Every product and service has competition. Customers are forced regularly to make decisions about what product or service is best for their business. Some of those decisions are based on price; some are based on relationships; and some are based on a rigorous and comparative analysis of the features, benefits, costs, and more. Somehow, customers ultimately decide whether to use your product or somebody else's.

In countless industries, customers perceive many of the products they purchase or use as virtually the same. When customers view products as similar, they must see the people selling them as different to make a choice. So, you really want to try to actually *be different*. Not to put too fine a point on it, the salesperson is part of the product or service offering and, ideally, adds unique and inimitable value. The salesperson can be part of (or be) the unassailable positioning.

Or not. If the customer sees a salesperson as interchangeable with all other salespeople and sees the products as generic or practically identical, a buying decision will probably be based on the lowest price. This is not the situation you want to be in.

I once asked a doctor which drug he prescribes for diabetes; he told me and then added that his former high school basketball coach represented his drug of choice. The likelihood I was going to sell this doctor my product was not very strong because of his long-standing relationship with the other rep. So I asked a question based on the unassailable position of my product, "Doctor, I look around your office and it seems to me that some of these people don't have much money. What percentage of the patients that you ordinarily treat with these kinds of products consider ten dollars a month a lot of money?"

He said half of them.

The product we represented was ten dollars a month less expensive than the one he was prescribing—my unassailable position. In that situation, the product I represented met the needs of those patients for whom ten bucks a month was a lot of money. And by using the words "[is] ten dollars a month a lot of money?" I caused the doctor to think about his patients in a new way—again, words matter.

Once you identify your position, you must be able to convey that message clearly to the customer. I communicated my company's price difference by asking questions about the doctor's patients. The questions I asked enabled him to think about the fact that he indeed had a place for my drug. In the process, I got half of his business.

Look at your accounts—do you have all the business that you should? Do you own a significant share of your potential business? Identify prospects where you should have business but do not; those buyers are where you are most likely to get new sales. Ask these questions to determine where your position is strongest:

- Do you know where your argument is strongest for a given product feature or customer?
- Do you know which prospects are the most likely to want your product or service?
- Have you framed your position so that it is unassailable?
- Have you formulated the questions so that they will likely get the customer to think about your positioning in a totally different but meaningful way?

156

Now, analyze selected prospects. Where is it obvious that you can win with them? If certain prospects are looking for a low-cost provider and you are a low-cost provider and they don't know it, then simply make them aware of your pricing and you will likely get that business—if price is their major buying motive.

With almost any product or service, there are places where you can win relatively easily. The trick is to identify those places and make those prospects aware of what you have to offer in a compelling way that makes them think. Because prospects are different, one position does not fit all. Once you understand what is important to your prospects, develop two or three powerful unassailable positions rooted in the facts where the logic is impeccable. Positioning your product this way will make it easy for prospects to see that this is the place where your product should be used. It also gives them solid information to defend the decision within their organization and, just as importantly, to a competitive salesperson who may also be a friend.

Questions are the most powerful way to establish unassailable positioning because they will get prospects to think about your product. Statements or presentations of fact do not guarantee the customer will think about the information. Once you ask the right questions and once you understand what your prospects and customers want, you can state your unassailable position. They will understand and you will have made it easy for them to decide to buy.

Selling is never easy and that is why we make buying easier when we can identify and effectively communicate our unassailable position. When we can get customers to think about our product differently, using impeccable logic that satisfies their genuine wants, we have probably made a sale using unassailable positioning.

USE A COMBINATION OF FACTS, BENEFITS, AND MORE

In the book, *Persuasion: The Art of Getting What You Want,* author, Dave Lakhani writes, "The challenge that many people have when they are persuading is that they do not take the time to think about what their story is. If you want to fly under your customer's radar or that of the people you are trying to persuade, then it is important that you tell a well-crafted story. Your story should be full of imagery and use powerful verbs to move the reader or listener. There is a big difference between a green sofa and an overstuffed chair with arms that come up to your ears when you sink into it with a child in your lap."

We can all recognize people who are great storytellers from those who can't tell a story, no matter how hard they try. Lakhani goes on to give us the steps to telling a persuasive story:

1. *Know your story.* The reason most of the stories you tell right now are not persuasive is that they have not been well thought out or the material and experience are not your own.

2. *Lay out your story.* A persuasive story answers the questions of who, what, where, why, and how in the following format:

- *Grab me by the ears.* You want a statement so powerful that people 15 feet away will stop what they are doing and come and listen or they will strain their ears and good manners to eavesdrop.

- *Lay the foundation.* In this section of your story, you lay the groundwork. You include any information customers must know to understand the story, fill in the holes in their knowledge, and give enough background so they can understand what you are saying.

- *Engage their emotions.* Get them excited or move them to a place where they are experiencing pain, lust, desire, or loss. . . . Be sure to use points that they will have a hard time disagreeing with or that they know immediately will happen to them or someone they know. As my partner Mike MacLeod says, "You want to know the prospect's pain, especially the pain they want to do something about soon. But then make sure you tell a story that reflects how you are going to try to eliminate or minimize the pain."

- *Layer on the proof.* Give customers an example featuring someone they know, preferably, or again, someone just like them. If you have no other reference, tell a story about yourself that adds credibility and proof.

- *Answer their questions.* Lay out at least three to five of the questions they will most likely have and answer them preemptively. Let them know that you are an expert because you know exactly what they have questions about.

- *Give them enough information that they can draw your conclusion.* Give them only enough detail so they have a few small questions left that require an interaction.

- *Get their feedback.* Customers want to know they got the point; they don't want to have to guess, so ask for reaction. Allow customers to give you more information now they have heard your story.

3. *Tell your story.* Telling your story is the fun part where most people fail. Think back to when you were a child and someone read to you. It was completely enthralling when someone who read a story could make the story come alive. Dragons roared, causing you to squeal in terror; maidens talked in high squeaky voices that tickled the insides of your ears, woodcutters' deep voices could rattle your bones. You were spellbound, and you couldn't wait for the next word. When your favorite reader was reading, you couldn't hear enough stories.

Persuasive storytellers engage your senses with their body language, their tone, their eye contact, and their emotions. They transfix you with emotion, tickle you with humor, and lead you to the only logical conclusion anyone could make.[1]

GIVE YOUR STORY BOTH LOGIC AND EMOTION

You need to have incredible clarity about the real differences between your product or service and those of your competitors. To benefit from this information, you must communicate *when those differences matter* using both logic and emotion. This point is significant because when you say to customers, "These are the differences in our product and here is when they matter for your situation . . ." the insinuation is that sometimes they don't matter. That is very credible. When you intimate that your product is not the greatest and latest and most wonderful, you are building credibility because the customer expects you to say otherwise.

Customers typically hear superlatives and absolutes from sales reps, and you know customers don't ordinarily believe or buy these claims. They accept real language that is minimal but believable. What you say is, "Here are the differences . . . and when do they matter?" and add immediately, "They matter in these two or three circumstances. Any other circumstances and they probably don't matter."

Salespeople often have a problem with this kind of language because they think that if they give something away by saying something good about the competitor or give the competitor a position, they are going to lose business. But the opposite usually happens. When you acknowledge your competitor's strengths, the credibility you build often will get you significantly more business than if you don't acknowledge your competitor's position—particularly if that position is valid.

This is not complex. If you don't deliver on Friday, and they do, but you deliver every other day including Saturday and they don't, then what you say is, "Use us Monday through Thursday and Saturday; use them on Friday." If the customer needs Friday deliveries, the customer *should* use them. I do not say you should get all the business; I say you should get all the business you deserve.

What business do you deserve? The answer to that goes back to the rigorous work you are doing on the concept of unassailable positioning and the development of your story. Determine where you have a match, and that's the business you deserve.

The way you present your product or services' differences becomes believable not by bashing the competition, but by giving the competition its due. In fact, when somebody says, "I use X company" or "I use Y product," the first words out of your mouth should be, "X company is a great company; that's a terrific product." The issue isn't whether it is a great company or whether it is a great product; the question is what are the differences and when (and if) do they matter? Therefore, the next thing you say is, "What I'd like to do is share with you some of the differences between that product and this and let's determine whether they matter for you."

This assumes you have such deep knowledge of the customer's business you can actually have an intelligent discussion about when the differences matter. It also means you must know your product and the competitor's so well that you can cobble together the differences and sound like a consultant not a salesperson.

There may be times when you don't have as much command of the competitive product(s) as you do your own and cannot make an objective, comparative analysis because you don't know enough. In that situation, you can ask. It is perfectly acceptable to say, "I'm not as familiar with that company as perhaps I should be. Would you mind telling me the things you like most about what they do and what you think makes their product or service unique? They may well have a better product or service than we do in some areas."

This is where *Your Story* comes in. The way you serve up the differences between your product and the other product is important because if you appear to be biased, if you wallow in the absolutes or the superlatives, you are not going to be seen as credible or different.

You need to clarify and verbalize why your company is different or how doing business with your company is different. For example, Nordstrom's return policy says it will take back any product without a receipt and with no hassles, whereas other department stores make returning merchandise a real pain. Look at your company through your customers' eyes and ask, what will the clients' experience be when they do business with our company? When you answer that question, you will have defined how your company is different.

Ask yourself: What is unique about our company? What makes us special and worthy of someone's business? There are usually significant differences between companies or the way they do business, or both. Think these through in detail and articulate them in such a way that customers or prospects truly understand what makes your company different. No two companies are alike and customers will do business with one based on its reputation, track record, and approach to business—but only if they know about it. The only way they will know is if you tell them.

BASE YOUR STORY ON A CUSTOMER WANT

To begin building your story, start with your unassailable positioning. You have identified your product's features and benefits, attributes, properties, and uniqueness. Now, you want to take those facts and begin weaving them into a story that is compelling and makes perfect sense to your customer. You must keep the customer engaged through its conclusion.

Far too often, salespeople take some sort of sales script or sales aid—a visual, a document, a testimonial, a flip chart—and simply try to explain it. They point out what this or that means. Many times, a salesperson will rely on the customer to connect the last few dots. Often, those last few dots make the difference between "good" and "compelling."

The first step in crafting your story is to define the fundamental hypothesis or premise that you are trying to advance. A premise is defined in the dictionary as, "a statement that is assumed to be true and from which a conclusion can be drawn." In a perfect setting, you are trying to get customers to listen to your story, to respond, and to give feedback to let you know whether it makes sense in this situation. So, your story must be rooted in some premise that makes a connection for them.

Your premise evolves from your unassailable position(s). You are looking to find people and companies that agree with your premise. The next step is *planned questions*. Even though you are telling your story, it is a two-way conversation. You want to find out if your clients agree, so you ask questions about the importance of your premise to their wants. If your unassailable position is that you can deliver precision-machined parts just in time for assembly into a final product, you should ask questions about the importance of just-in-time delivery to the prospect's company and its impact on the financial bottom line. Here are a few sample questions:

- What role does just-in-time delivery play in the ultimate success of your factory?
- How exactly do you and your company define just-in-time delivery?

- What happens to morale when parts are not available?
- If you had to guess, what might be the financial impact to your organization if you were better able to plan production with the sure knowledge that the parts you need would be available when you needed them?

Note that these questions include both logic and emotion—just-in-time delivery can be financially quantified and it can improve morale.

Once you have the answers to these questions, you will know whether the position makes sense for prospects. If it is obvious that they do not agree, then your firm's ability to deliver just in time for assembly is not a match for them and you should move on. If there is agreement, you can advance to the next step—*cascading logic.*

Cascading logic is the point at which you talk about your product or service's unassailable position. It is the step during which you address all the wants and needs you have uncovered with your questions by telling your product's unique story.

As you are talking and sharing your logic, you want it to be interesting; it should be true and relevant. Your story should also be engaging, clear, and should be rooted in real facts about your product. You may even be in a position to compare your product with a competitor's.

If you find yourself discussing a competitor, avoid an "Us versus Them" mentality. This could cause customers to become defensive, particularly if they are currently using the competitive product. Instead, focus your efforts on your product position: why it is best; why other people have found it to be beneficial. Your positioning shows where your product fits best—not why the competitor's product is ineffectual.

Keep it clear. Too often when salespeople explain a product or a service to someone they think knows something about the subject, they use shortcuts, acronyms, and jargon. This can diminish the story's clarity. Benefits that seem blindingly obvious to you may not be clear to someone else, even to someone whom you think is knowledgeable about the issues involved.

Keep it simple. We tend to believe that people think in specific intellectual business terms, but the truth is most of us think most clearly in simple terms, with simple stories and analogies. Therefore, the story has to be powerful, it has to be well prepared, it has to be so well thought-out that the customer says (or thinks), "Wow! I never thought of it that way!" Ideally, it engenders thinking.

Consider telling your story as if you were telling it to your mother or a favorite aunt who knows nothing about your business. If you had to explain to your mother why your product is appropriate in a given situation, what would you say? How would you explain to her that this is actually a sound choice?

HELP CUSTOMERS SEE THERE IS MINIMAL RISK

Most businesspeople dislike surprises. They hate unpleasant surprises—a missed delivery, a quality glitch, a cost overrun. Most don't even like pleasant surprises. It is part of the salesperson's job to ensure that there are no nasty surprises and that buying the company's product or service has minimal risk and large potential gain.

There may be times, however, when a surprise is appropriate. A sales representative once told me about a customer he had approached with all his logic but she wasn't using any of his product. He asked me what to do. I said: "The first thing you have to do is go and apologize to her." He asked what I meant, "apologize?" I said: "Your approach is all wrong. If she is not using your product, your approach is wrong. From what you described to me, she is someone who would probably see you as a seller who is interested in himself. So my suggestion is apologize to her, tell her your approach was wrong, and you are not there to try to get her business but you want to get back on the right foot. You want to provide service and value to her. If at some point in the future she wants to have a dialogue about your product and where it fits, you would like to do that but for now you want to get off the wrong foot."

The point is, he was trying to sell her; and in trying with impeccable logic and his passion, he had come across as being too aggressive, too pushy, and not understanding her needs. When he apologized and said, "I don't care if I ever get your business, but I do care about repairing this relationship," over time he wound up getting half her business.

Mike Bradley, the general manager of Derse, Pittsburgh, and a vice president of the parent corporation says, "Let me understand that customer and that customer's business so there are no surprises. We are preparing for a presentation, and I saw on the ticker tape that the customer just got approval on an acquisition. You better believe that is going to be part of the presentation, because now they have to take that client's brand and product into the marketing mix."

Derse builds trade show exhibits, and Mike says that the acquired company probably had shows to appear at. The knowledge of the acquisition and incorporating it into the presentation "hopefully is enough for the client to recognize that this is a thinking organization. It has to be massive challenges for the marketing team and the sales team to integrate all that. Being in alignment with your clients' goals and understanding is powerful."

YOUR STORY NEEDS TO BE TRUE

This is not a point I need to belabor for the readers of this book. Remember that even a small white lie can bite you. Greg Genova, who sells cutting tools for Kennametal in California, says: "The first thing is you always have to be truthful. You have to be, because you will get caught so quickly if you promise them something you can't deliver or do something that is unethical—they will remember that forever."

A compelling story communicates exactly where your product or service fits best and how that logic is supported from a practical perspective. The story needs to be rooted in some fundamental hypothesis based on the attributes of the brand as it relates to competitors. The story is best built around unassailable truths (facts about the product that cannot be denied) and should include logic and emotion. The story should be focused on one or more of the three things customers in this business or industry want. And lastly, you should know your three or four stories so well you can do them in your sleep.

CHAPTER 8

ASK FOR A COMMITMENT

The final step in the DELTA process is to ask for a commitment. This step is often called "the close." Is anything more important to a sales call than the close? Has any sales topic been written about more? Closing, after all, is the skill most sales managers feel their salespeople need to work on to be more effective.

Historically, the sales close has been one of the more overtly manipulative skills managers and sales trainers have taught their reps. Different closes have acquired names: the assumptive close, the choice close, the success story close, the contingent close, the counterbalance close, the boomerang close, the stimulus-response close, the minor points close, the standing-room-only close, the impending event close, the puppy dog close, the ask-for-the-order close, the order form close, the summary close, the special-deal close, the no-risk close, the turnover close, the pretend-to-leave close, and the ask-for-help close.

We're not going to talk about these closing techniques because (1) you can look them up in any good personal selling textbook, and (2) *a close is nothing more than a commitment to do something beyond that to which the prospect has already committed or is already doing.*

This is the great rub. Many good sales interactions happen on a day-to-day basis. Sales reps have reasonable dialogues, good conversations, and the opportunity to present their story; and they do so in a credible, compelling fashion. Then at meeting's end, the story sometimes seems to just fall apart because it has not been tied together tightly with an appropriate close.

It falls apart because, as psychological tests have demonstrated, both buyers and sellers become different at the point of closing than they were during the rest of a sales call. Something happens emotionally that causes prospects to feel differently about what salespeople are about to ask them to do.

This may be anxiety driven by buyer's remorse or concern for impulse buying. Have I had ample time to make this decision? Do I know this rep well enough to trust her? Is this really a good decision?

For salespeople, the anxiety is driven by the fact that the close is the moment of truth: If I don't get the order now, I'm never going to get it. Or: I don't want the rejection. This opportunity for rejection is perhaps the biggest bugaboo of them all.

We have found an interesting phenomenon. Ask a group of salespeople who do not have their sales manager in the room to raise their hands if they agree with this statement: "I am more likely to ask a closing question when my boss is with me than when I am by myself." All hands go up. Every time. Why is that so?

Salespeople know their bosses expect them to ask a closing question. They know they have to ask a closing question to be seen as doing their jobs properly. At the same time, they are often not comfortable asking a closing question. If they were comfortable, they would ask when the boss wasn't watching. Why are most salespeople uncomfortable asking closing questions on a routine basis?

They are uncomfortable because most closing questions they've learned over the years are inconsistent with who they see themselves as human beings. If you do not want to be an aggressive, pushy person, you are not going to feel comfortable asking what you think are aggressive, pushy questions. These are questions like, "Do you want delivery on Thursday or Friday?" (the choice close) or "If I can show you how your company can reduce production costs by 20 percent without losing quality, will you buy?" (the contingent close).

Most of us are not aggressive by nature. Most of us are not pushy, but the closing questions we've been taught are often offensive not only to us, but also to our prospects. We can frequently see it in their expressions and body language. If a question offends the questioner and makes customers visibly uncomfortable, it may explain why many salespeople will not ask the question except under pressure. Why deliberately and knowingly make somebody uncomfortable? Especially if you want—or need—their cooperation?

If these are the problems with closing, what is the answer? The answer is to focus less on closing than on obtaining a commitment. *A commitment is the appropriate end to the current conversation.* It is not necessarily an order, although it may be. But the commitment may be only for another meeting. It may be to meet this person's boss. It may be permission to leave your equipment with the organization for a month.

With that definition in mind let's consider the six principles of asking for a commitment:

1. People are far more likely to change behavior if you ask for a commitment than if you do not.

2. Commitment questions need to be comfortable for you and the prospect/customer.

3. Great commitments start with precall planning.

4. Sensory trial closes make commitment questions easy to ask.

5. Commitments are the natural, appropriate end to a conversation.

6. Asking for the seriousness of the commitment after someone makes a commitment is perfectly acceptable and will increase your sales if you do it well.

Let's look at each one of these in some detail.

COMMITMENTS CHANGE PEOPLE'S BEHAVIOR

There is an incredible power in getting a commitment—any commitment. People's behavior is in line with the verbal commitments they make; most people will make an effort to do what they say they will do (those who will not make the effort do not make good customers . . . or good friends). People are far more likely to change behavior if you ask for a commitment than if you do not. Very often, however, salespeople ask for a very large commitment, and, almost always, requests for large commitments cause resistance and lead to very small behavior changes. The reverse is also true: if you ask for a small commitment, prospects are more likely to act on it because they perceive the commitment as reasonable.

So, you might ask a customer to try your product for a week or a month. Or in the case of a training program, you might ask customers to try one pilot program and see how it fits. Something like this is more likely to engender large behavior change, because if the product does what the salesperson said it does, then customers are more likely to continue with it in a big way.

A company once asked me to create a sales message for a new product launch. The initial introduction was in October with a second launch into another market two months later. The company hired me to speak at the first launch meeting, before they had seen me do my work. I said that if it made sense for me to speak at the first meeting, I ought to do it for the next meeting as well.

My contact said he wanted to see how well I did at the first meeting before committing to a second. I asked for a commitment, which I thought made sense, and I didn't get it.

My charge was to give a one-hour speech before 300 people. At the end of the speech, they gave me a lengthy standing ovation. When I made it to the back of the room, the person who hired me for the speech and to whom I had submitted the proposal for the second meeting hugged me. I whispered in his ear, "I guess now's a good time to ask you to sign that other contract," and he said, "Consider it signed."

Commitments change behavior: In particular they change the behavior of customers and salespeople. Customers are more likely to do what they say they are going to do; when you do what you say you are going to do, they are more likely to want to do more of what you want them to do.

Notice the dual commitment here. You make a commitment to deliver first-rate work and first-rate service. The customer commits to compensating you. Once you get the business, extending it and asking for additional commitments requires a commitment on your part. The commitment I had to make was to deliver first-quality work. That changed the customer's behavior and his willingness to make a commitment in response to my commitment to excellence.

It is important to keep your radar tuned into earning the right to ask for the commitment. You will have to judge that right based on the quality of the interaction you had with the other person. You need to sense that the hypothesis or premise you are advancing is actually resonating and making some sense to the customer. This requires you to listen.

"I think listening skills are really the Achilles heel of salespeople—especially young folks," says Shari Kulkis at Roche. "They are ingrained in the sales process and using the ACR Method—Acknowledge, Clarify, and Respond—and following a certain route of thinking, but they are not listening. They are thinking about what they want to get out to the person, the message they want to convey. They are interested in their own interests. When you really listen to what a person is saying, you can find out what their needs are, what their issues are, what their concerns are, and what their objections are. If you are not listening, you miss it and how you respond ends up not fulfilling their need. The bottom line is they don't buy."

Professor Dan Weilbaker at Northern Illinois University would agree with Shari. He says he has been looking for years for ways to teach people to listen better. "I give a lot of verbal directions and assignments for the students to realize they have to listen to get it right, and to understand what I am saying. I don't ask them, 'Do you understand?' They have two options. One, they can come ask me about it, or they can go ahead and do what they think they need to do. If they do what they think they need to do and it's wrong, that is going to impact their grade. Most students will complain and I will use that opportunity to reinforce that they didn't listen. You need to listen, and if you don't understand, you ask."

The sales program at Northern Illinois University includes role-playing that the teachers videotape. Seeing themselves on tape, students start to realize the things they missed during their interactions. They can watch themselves without being under pressure. "That is usually an eye-opener for a lot of them," says Dan. "It's, 'Oh my God, the customer was saying this, and I completely blanked on it.' They can see the importance of listening and how much it will help them. In role-playing, I have said, 'I would really like to have this product,' and they are off telling me something else. Then they see the tape and say, 'You told me you wanted it, and I didn't even ask you!' I think that helps, but I still haven't found a good way to help students learn to listen better."

Questions are really a subset of listening. Great listeners are people who ask great questions because they do listen. They not only hear the words, they understand the meaning, nuance, and implications of what the person is saying—or if they don't understand, they ask questions that help them truly comprehend. The marriage of great listening with great questioning leads to great understanding.

Dan says listening attentively is very difficult for students and salespeople. "If I were a sales manager," he says, "I would be working with the salespeople and illustrate what they missed by not listening. Debrief them after a call to ask, 'Did you hear the customer say this? What does it mean? How did you interpret it? What's going on here?' Try to see there are things prospects say you can get clues from." One of the clues can be that you are talking to the wrong person.

Never underestimate the importance of a commitment. You need to ask a commitment question whether your manager is present or not because these questions dramatically impact people's behavior. Once again, you must consider putting your customer at ease. Find questions that are easy for you to ask and that the customer is comfortable answering, like, "Does what we have discussed today sound like a reasonable approach? Would you be willing to give us a fair trial?" Now listen for a response before speaking again. No matter how difficult that is to do.

COMMITMENT QUESTIONS NEED TO BE COMFORTABLE

One of the keys to quality closing is making sure you are comfortable asking the closing questions. Commitment questions need to be comfortable for you and for the prospect or customer. If you are uncomfortable, your behavior will make the customer uneasy. The commitment should seem like a reasonable and feasible request from the customer's perspective and not just your perspective.

Closing begins with your mind-set. This anxiety I have been discussing occurs because salespeople traditionally treat "*the close*" as a one-time event. They think they are expected to get that piece of business in that moment, or there will be hell to pay back at the office. The close is really part of a process. It may or may not culminate in a sale at that particular moment or on that particular day. If your mind-set is right and you have thought out your plan, you will know if your objective today is to move forward in the process or get the customer to sign on the dotted line. There should not be any anxiety, just comfortable questions that lead you from one step to the next by virtue of meaningful conversation.

So, you must begin well in advance of the close. The environment you establish from the opening of your call has tremendous bearing on how your closing will feel to you and the customer. If closing begins with the first words you utter in a sales conversation (and it does), it is vitally important that you have great clarity about what you want to happen with this interaction. This kind of clarity occurs during your planning. Determine your specific objective for the meeting—what do you want to happen? It may be to close the sale but it could also be to learn more about the prospect's needs, the company's buying process, or this person's place in the hierarchy. Your ultimate objective may be to set up another meeting. The point is (and you have heard it before), you must *plan* the interaction. It can change during the meeting because interactions by their nature are fluid. Sometimes you learn that things have changed since your last visit, so you need to have a degree of flexibility about changing what you are asking a person to do.

Remember: Selling is nothing more than finding someone with an open mind, willing to have a conversation, believing there might be some mutual benefit in what you have to offer. Try to understand their situation and obtain clarity and agreement before you present your hypothesis. Prospects give you feedback on whether what you are saying makes sense. If, at the end of the session, the hypothesis you are advancing seems to make sense, you can ask: "How does that sound?"

Without promoting customer commitments for further visits to their quarterly trunk sales (and referrals), a Doncaster direct sales representative's business would soon dry up. Lesley Boyer, now president and CEO of The Sterling Edge in San Clemente, California, has been a successful Doncaster representative. Lesley says her role was to help customers buy and to encourage a commitment to return. As an example, Lesley tells the story of a new client, Sharon.

Like 70 percent of Lesley's business, Sharon was a referral. As a referral, and because Lesley qualified her on the phone, Sharon was aware of Doncaster's approximate prices. She told Lesley she was taking a year off from her career and said, "I want to start over. I want you to completely redo me."

Lesley tells me, "The initial feeling is dollar signs in the eyes, like Scrooge McDuck, and that's a real risk. I don't want that kind of power. I figure by the time she is ten, a young woman pretty well knows what she wants, and Sharon was more than ten. I told her, we have to think about this." Sharon asked what color Lesley thought would look good on her. Sharon was a dark-eyed brunette with alabaster skin. Lesley said, "Red. And I have a beautiful red blazer right here. I think you said you like a longer jacket, finger-tip length." Leslie handed it to her and said, "Try this on."

Sharon put it on and said, "Yuck!"

"Tell me what you see," said Lesley. "Tell me about the other bright colors you have in your closet."

Sharon paused and said, "I don't have any."

"So you see," Lesley told her, "you don't have any red in your closet, so even though I think red might be a great color on you, it doesn't matter what I think. You are the one who's going to be wearing it, and if you don't have red in your closet now, there's no reason you should start. I don't want the responsibility of telling you what you should be wearing, because these clothes will sit in your closet and then you'll be upset with me. I want you back, and I want your referrals. So let's talk about what you already have, and let's just add to it. Rather than start over, we'll add some pieces today. There are four trunk shows a year, so next time you can add more pieces from them."

Lesley accomplished several objectives. She assured Sharon that just because she had money for a completely new wardrobe, she didn't need one. She helped Sharon buy at this initial appointment, but even more importantly she also obtained a commitment from Sharon to return for future trunk shows. In fact, Sharon did come to Lesley's shows two or three times a year for several years even after she became pregnant and had two more children.

GREAT COMMITMENTS START WITH PRECALL PLANNING

The best commitment questions are planned in advance and are a natural progression of your story, which ultimately leads to a closing. Precall planning is not a stagnant process; it's fluid. Part of Tim Wackel's precall planning is to be prepared for anything. If the sale stalls or inertia appears in the middle of what looks like a promising sale, his plan is to nudge the customer gently. "Sometimes everything sounds good, and then all of a sudden prospects just kind of disappear," says Tim. "They don't return my phone calls and they don't reply to my e-mails. I understand that people get busy, and I am not at the top of their to-do list. There is food and survival and family and financial freedom and vacation planning. But if the meetings felt good and I've given them sufficient time and I've reached out and they haven't gotten back to me, I'll send a final communication."

Typically this will be an e-mail, sometimes a voice mail, says Tim. He apologizes for having taken the prospect's time, then continues, "Our earlier conversations led me to believe that there was a lot of interest on your part. I felt like we had a viable solution. I thought we were moving toward getting something to happen. But your lack of responsiveness indicates to me that either the problem has gone away, you have found somebody else to do this, or this is no longer a priority. I want to demonstrate my persistence, but I don't want to become a pest, so I am going to wait to hear back from you. We will discontinue our efforts to connect with you unless you reach out to us."

The tone is apologetic—we are sorry we wasted your time. The message is factual—we thought things were on track . . . here are the assumptions we made . . . your lack of responsiveness tells us something has changed. Tim says that more often than not he receives an e-mail within hours saying something like, "No, hold it, stop. I am so sorry. Things have gotten busy. There has been a reorganization, I've had some personal problems at home."

Virtually always, the prospect cites some compelling event that prevented an earlier response. Usually, says Tim, "the client or the prospect comes back saying, 'I'm so sorry. Yes, I've been getting your messages. I've been reading your e-mails and I have just been too busy to reply, but please, please don't disengage.' Once I say I don't want to bother them any more, they say they're still interested."

Tim says that in his experience, most salespeople will continue to leave messages and send e-mails indefinitely. "I teach salespeople you can build a career by finding yeses and nos. Both are great answers, and 'yes' is a better answer than 'no,' but both are fine. 'Maybe' will suck the life out of you. Get prospects to say 'yes,' or let them have permission to say 'no.' But unresponsive, unclear, inaccurate communication just kills time." And don't forget a commitment from a customer can be "no" and that's not bad either.

SENSORY TRIAL CLOSES MAKE COMMITMENT QUESTIONS EASY

One of the easiest ways to be comfortable with your closing questions is to use the sensory trial close. The sensory trial close is a technique for creating closing questions that use the words *who, what, where, why, how much,* and *when* in combination with sensory words like *look, think, touch, sound, feel,* and *view.* When you ask questions in this format, people are usually very comfortable answering and you should be at ease asking them. Before asking the commitment question, it is a good idea to ask a "sensory" agreement question. Here are some examples:

- How does that sound?
- If it makes any sense, over the next couple of weeks, when you have an opportunity to use something like this, will you consider giving us a try?
- Does this logic speak to you?
- Does this seem like a reasonable way to look at it?
- In your point of view, does what we have discussed sound like something that would fit with what you are doing?

183

- I feel like we have accomplished everything that we agreed to, so how would you suggest we move forward?
- How do you feel about what we've discussed today?

This is a process of discovery. What you are trying to do is uncover the reality of the situation. Do they understand your hypothesis? Is your hypothesis so compelling and the situation so genuine that now is the time to act? You may identify situations, problems, and challenges that prospects *say* they want to solve, but in truth they don't want to solve them. If they do, they don't want to solve them now or they are way down on a list of priorities. Part of what salespeople have to learn as they go through this process is whether this difficulty (or opportunity) seems important enough to the buyer to act now. And if not now, when?

By asking buyers, "How does that sound?" you gain valuable insight into how they view your hypothesis. So, what kind of answer can you expect to hear? We hear only two answers to that question: "Yes, it sounds good" or, "Yes, it sounds good . . . but . . . ." *We rarely—if ever—hear "No."*

"Yes . . . but," is effectively "No." Nevertheless, "Yes . . . but" is usually the prospects' opportunity to explain the flaws they see in your fundamental logic. Or the issues they see that remain as impediments to completing the transaction.

If you ask, "How does that sound?" and they say, "It sounds great," they are signaling that you now have the right to find out if they are ready to buy. A couple of questions that you might ask are, "If it sounds great, is it fair to ask you to try it? Is it fair that I ship you 20 of these by next Thursday?" In other words, if they have sanctioned your hypothesis, they are giving you implied permission to take the next step.

If they say, "It sounds great . . . but," the "but" becomes the most important part of the sale: But . . . we are already over-stocked. But . . . I am still worried about your price. But . . . we have never done business with you before. But . . . you are not in our system. But . . . we only have one vendor. But . . . I am not the only decision maker.

The world of sales is full of "buts." They are important factors that often get you closer to the sale because they tend to reveal the genuine reasons why someone is not ready to complete the transaction or buy. When you meet a "but" (another word for an objection) during a sales conversation, do three things:

1. *Acknowledge:* Make certain you acknowledge the concern or issue and show understanding. The worst thing you can do is press on, ignoring or dismissing the customer's concern.

2. *Clarify:* Either restate what you heard in a way that captures the essence of the concern or, if it is not clear, ask clarifying questions to gain deeper understanding. Salespeople, hypersensitive to customer concerns, sometimes answer another objection entirely. Don't assume you know what the customer is getting at without more information.

3. *Respond:* Reframe the issue or deal with misperceptions.

Henry Potts at Melillo Consulting suggests that when good salespeople meet an objection, such as, "We don't have the money now," they continue probing. What is the cost of doing nothing? Focus on whether the product or service will improve the prospect's overall cost structure. "Any CEO running a company, any kind of a company," says Henry, "cares about reducing costs, becoming more efficient, increasing sales, or all three. The ideal is to do all three. Every salesperson who has a message to deliver at that level needs to be able to deliver it in that context. It's not about: Do you have the budget for it? It's about making an investment on your part so you get a return and ultimately you need to spend less money overall."

COMMITMENTS ARE THE APPROPRIATE END TO A CONVERSATION

We close every conversation. Sometimes it is as bland as, "Talk to you tomorrow," "See you later," or "I'll call you on Monday," but, as with these phrases, we often close the conversation with a commitment. It is something we do naturally, although we may not always want a formal commitment: "I will call you at 2:30 on Monday. Does that work for you?"

This is one of the problems salespeople often have: they think every interaction with a customer must end with a formal commitment of some kind. A conversation demands an appropriate close and that may lead to—or be—a commitment, but is not necessarily one.

Interacting with customers is a dynamic process. I had a conversation recently with a prospect with whom I am trying to close a deal. I asked a friend of mine to have the prospect call me from the golf course. For me, it was a sales interaction. But it was also touching base. I said, "How are you doing? What's going on? I haven't heard from you in a while."

He said, "You know we announced some changes today and I need to talk to you because we're going to need to engage your services."

I said he should call me, closing the conversation without asking for any commitment. A week later, I sent him an e-mail giving him my travel schedule and suggesting a date I could meet with him if he were available; or, I asked, are talks still premature? I still had not asked for a commitment.

Five minutes later, I received an e-mail from him saying he had already told his sales team the company was going to engage our services and that he would get back to me about the date I'd suggested. I am going to have to ask for a commitment at some point, but not every sales interaction requires a commitment to close appropriately.

Closing appropriately is exactly that: having clarity about what you are trying to accomplish and making sure that you end the conversation appropriately. Ending appropriately may mean that you have to create some action to further the sales process. A good closing or commitment question should seek a specific action or new behavior to which the customer is likely to agree because it makes perfect sense in light of what you have just discussed, and does not seem unreasonable or greedy to the customer. Don't ask for all the business, just that part you deserve based on your conversation.

ASK FOR THE SERIOUSNESS OF THE COMMITMENT

Asking for the seriousness of the commitment after someone makes one is perfectly acceptable and will increase your sales if you do it well.

Here's an example of what not to do: An acquaintance I had not talked to for two years sent me an e-mail then called me on the phone: "We need to talk . . . we've got to have you . . . send me a proposal." I spent an hour on the phone with him and spent two or three hours creating a proposal, but I never asked him about the seriousness of his commitment. I made the assumption because of the tone and the nature of our dialogue and the e-mail that he was serious.

It was a huge mistake on my part because I have not heard from him since. I've left him three or four messages; I've sent three or four e-mails; I've sent text messages, and gotten nothing from him.

Because he sounded serious, I didn't test the seriousness of his commitment. I should have said something like, "I'm getting the impression from this conversation that my creating a proposal fairly rapidly is important to you, and that if I create the proposal—and we're not miles apart in terms of the budget—you're going to act on it. Is that a fair assumption?" At that point, he would have told me, "Yes, that's a fair assumption," or "No, we're just in the early stages," or "The budget's really a big deal." Or something else that meant "No."

Unfortunately, many people don't have the backbone to tell you they're in the early stages of the buying process. Or tell you they're shopping around. Or, in a misguided attempt to be nice, they say, "Yes, send me a proposal."

I have salespeople regularly tell me, "I called on this person. It was a great call. They seemed interested. They asked me to send them a proposal, and then I never heard from them."

I tell them that they didn't test the seriousness of the prospect's commitment. If someone says they're committed, you have every right to ask, "How serious is your commitment? Is it serious enough for me to create a proposal [or arrange scheduling or order parts or do whatever your organization will have to do as the next step]? I am willing to go through these actions to do this, but I'm only doing that because I believe that what you're saying to me is that there's a high degree of likelihood that you and I are going to do business together. If I have misread it, then please set the record straight for me."

When you take the closing to that next level, testing the seriousness of the commitment, you will increase your closing ratios dramatically because you'll weed out the people who aren't really serious. You'll learn that what they said isn't really what they meant. You'll find people who will say to you: "I'm not the decision maker. I think this is exactly what we've got to do, so give me the proposal and I'll go to bat for you."

They just told me I'm talking to the wrong person. Now, rather than spending my time creating a proposal, I need to find the right person. My next step in the process isn't to do the proposal and hope for the business. My next step is to find somebody who is both serious about the commitment and can make it.

You have to be aware of your own assumptions, and then test them on the prospect. Valerie Sokolosky's mistake in negotiating (as she recognized) was assuming that the budget was not going to be a problem, but she didn't test that assumption with the prospect (see Chapter 5). There's nothing wrong with saying something like: "May I assume you have a budget for this engagement. Could you share with me what that is?" Then stop and listen.

When you test the seriousness of someone's commitment, if you find them backing up if the commitment isn't serious. And when you find them backing up, you know you do not yet have the business.

Far too often, salespeople don't test the seriousness of a prospect's commitment. It is one of the most overlooked aspects of selling. At the same time, the most inappropriate way to ask for a commitment is by asking the traditional closing questions that make you uncomfortable. If you really want to increase your success, test the seriousness of someone's commitment. And you have every right to do that.

Sometimes people say to me, "Send me a proposal." I usually say, "I don't do proposals. I have told you what it costs. I have told you what we're going to do. I have outlined our process. Why would I need to do a proposal? If you tell me that if I send you a proposal you're going to sign it, I'll be happy to write it." Ninety percent of the time, that works; 10 percent of the time, you send a proposal and you don't get the business.

But if the customer and I have had a meaningful dialogue, I've learned the situation, I've explained what our projects usually cost in terms of a range, and they're serious about a commitment, I feel comfortable saying I'm not writing a proposal.

Most people who make a serious commitment will keep it. There's incredible power in commitments. But there's a difference between a soft and a hard commitment. A soft commitment generates soft results. Hard commitments generate hard results. I always want to turn a soft commitment into a hard commitment.

Most salespeople are happy with a soft commitment, because it's the eureka! I've done my job. But you haven't done your job until the customer places an order. If you want to increase the likelihood that you'll get the business, turn your soft commitments into hard commitments, by testing the customer's seriousness.

Encouraging a solid commitment requires four things:

1. Establishing a positive mind-set and fully understanding what you need to accomplish to move prospects or customers forward.

2. Planning and crafting the right questions and closing or thinking about the questions in advance of the closing process (or the next step process) in such a way that you are comfortable asking the question. Make sure you feel good about the questions you plan to ask.

3. Stating your hypothesis and asking questions so that prospects or clients will not be offended, but will see this as a logical next part of this discussion.

4. Listening to their response. It may or may not be an order—and that's all right. It's not a rejection; it's a continuing part of a process.

Remember, the close is not always the end of business; it can be the continuation of business or the discussion. Closing is a process. But even the best sales process can be improved by building positive business relationships.

SECTION III

IMPLEMENT THE PROCESS FOR PERSONAL PROSPERITY

CHAPTER 9

HOW TO BUILD POSITIVE, PRODUCTIVE BUSINESS RELATIONSHIPS

When I ask senior executives what role positive, productive business relationships play in their salespeople's efforts, they inevitably tell me that relationships are crucial. When I ask how they train their salespeople to build relationships with people they don't naturally connect with, they say they don't. This is a huge disconnect in my mind: if building productive relationships is crucial, we need to learn how to do it.

I have stressed that salespeople require three components for success: the right mind-set, an effective sales process, and strong business relationships. Without all three, it is difficult, if not impossible, to reach your full potential in sales. We have discussed mind-set and laid out the DELTA sales process. Because relationships matter so much in selling, how do you go about building positive, productive business relationships?

As a salesperson, you grow in your career as you expand and improve your network of relationships with customers and prospects (and with coworkers, managers, and others key to your success). If you have superior relationships that you nurture and leverage with all your key business contacts, you will, almost automatically, be more successful in your business life. Certainly the converse is true. When you have poor relationships with customers, coworkers, and managers, your business life suffers (not to mention your personal life).

This chapter is based heavily on *The Relationship Edge: The Key to Strategic Influence and Selling Success,* 2nd edition by Jerry Acuff with Wally Wood (Hoboken, NJ: John Wiley & Sons, 2007).

Building business relationships consciously, systematically, routinely, and proactively is a skill anyone can learn. I have been teaching it to salespeople for several years, and I know it works. It is a process you can easily master because, if you have a best friend or spouse, you already know instinctively what the process requires. Adopt the process outlined here, and your business (and personal) relationships will improve—I have seen it happen hundreds of times with salespeople I have managed and counseled. I have learned that the people who are greatest at this are the ones who do it proactively. Sadly, most people approach relationships reactively.

A strong, positive relationship changes the dynamic between you and another person. When your relationship is weak, for example, the customer's statement, "I can't talk to you today," may mean, "I don't want to talk to you—at all . . . ever." When your relationship is strong, however, the identical statement, "I can't talk to you today," means only, "I can't talk to you today." You know there's no hidden rejection lurking under the words because you have a positive relationship. You know you're not being brushed off. You also know that next week you can talk for an hour if needed. *Identical words have different meanings based on your relationship.* With a valued business relationship, you function in a far more productive environment where you and the customer feel safe sharing the truth.

CLIMB THE RELATIONSHIP PYRAMID

There are five positive relationship levels you can have with another human being (illustrated in Figure 9.1). They form a Re-

Figure 9.1
The Relationship Pyramid

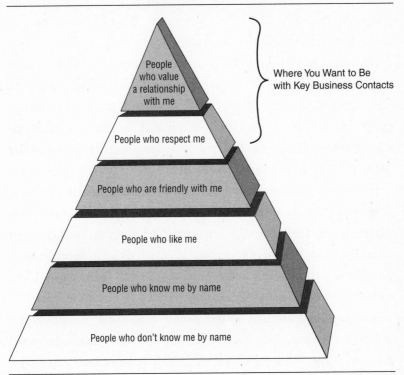

lationship Pyramid because a great many people, literally billions, form the base—the people who do not even know you by name—and relatively few are at the peak—the people who value a relationship with you.

It is relatively easy to move up from the base to the level where people know you by name. And the best way to have people remember your name, as you probably know, is to use and know their name.

The next level up includes the people who know you by name and who like you; they don't mind your being around. They are not offended when you visit. You are not close to them, but they've left the door ajar to becoming closer.

The next level covers the people who are friendly; they will talk about more than the immediate business at hand. They will chat about the football game or weekend plans or vacation events. At this level, you have established and are sharing common interests and concerns, and you now routinely talk about them whenever you are together.

The level just below the top of the Relationship Pyramid consists of the people who respect you, which the dictionary defines as "esteem for or a sense of the worth or excellence of a person, a personal quality, or ability." People who respect you have a high opinion of your integrity, your knowledge, your courage, or all three.

The top level consists of the people who value a relationship with you, because they believe it is in *their* best interest to have one. (*You* may believe it's in their best interest to have a relationship with you, but if they don't agree, it doesn't count.) They trust you, think you can help them, and are confident you will not abuse their trust. Even better, the feeling is mutual; just as you help people at the top of the pyramid, they will help you.

Most business relationships are at the Know-Me-By-Name/Like-Me/Friendly-With-Me levels. These are all about likability. Asking the right questions will cause almost anybody to like you reasonably quickly. The most effective way to get people to like you is to get them to talk about themselves and the things they treasure.

Just to be liked is not enough, however. When you reach the top two levels on The Relationship Pyramid, you have relationships that can help you reach even your stretch goals. But how do you get people to respect you and how do you get people to value a relationship with you? You need a relationship-building process: an understanding of human beings and ways to gain respect. You can also map your relationships and hop from one pyramid to another. These powerful concepts are how relationships can change your lot in life.

The process has three steps:

1. What you think.
2. What you ask.
3. What you do.

Like many things in life, this is a lot easier to talk about than actually do.

HAVE THE RIGHT MIND-SET

By now you know I am certain that what you think drives your actions. You must believe relationships will benefit you, that if you work to build your business relationships, you will be rewarded. You must believe you are someone with whom prospects and customers would want to have a relationship because you have experience, training, skills, abilities, knowledge (or all five) that they value. You must also think well of others and learn to think as much as you can from the other person's point of view.

As Buddha said centuries ago, "What we think, we become." If you walk into a meeting knowing (because your predecessor told you) that this prospect dislikes salespeople, you are likely to find someone who dislikes salespeople. If, however, you walk into the same meeting believing you can build a positive, productive relationship with just about anybody (regardless of what your predecessor told you), the odds are good you will have an encouraging experience. In our relationships, both business and personal, we tend to find what we expect to find. If we expect to find prospects brusque, impersonal, and hard-nosed, that's what we tend to find. If we expect to find them interesting, friendly, and flexible, that's what we tend to find.

Mutual respect is crucial in building winning relationships and creating an atmosphere of comfort. When you meet someone for the first time, that person probably feels fairly neutral about you. From your first action—a firm handshake—and your first words, the person begins to form an opinion that either holds you in respect or does not. Often we do and say things that others don't respect. We're late. We're unprepared. We appear to be biased.

Another important consideration is how you view yourself. Some people don't like themselves because they are overweight, or have a bad complexion, or are shy. They wish they could change things they don't like about themselves, but they don't change and so they beat themselves up for not changing. A certain amount of self-acceptance must take place before you will be effective in developing relationships. Most of us are harder on ourselves than anybody we will ever meet (possibly excluding our families).

To function effectively, you must accept that you are doing your best. If you're truly not doing your best, you probably don't respect yourself as much as you should. In that case, you should do what is necessary to change. Try to correct what you do wrong, but don't overreact because you made a mistake. Don't lie. Keep your word. Do what you say you are going to do and accept that all you can ever do is your best.

You must also think well of others even when, on the surface, they are not likable. When I was a district manager for a certain pharmaceutical company, I competed with Dick McDonald, then a district manager in Detroit. I never liked being around him because I thought we were completely different people. We had different likes and dislikes. In addition, we competed with one another. We were both district managers, both wanted to have the top district, both wanted to be promoted, I felt the natural competition one feels with one's peers that exists in any business—but perhaps I felt it more than was healthy. One day, my boss mentioned Dick McDonald, and I remarked, "I don't like Dick McDonald. He's a jerk."

He said, "Well, that's an interesting point of view." He thought about it for a minute, then said, "Here's what I want you to do. You go to Detroit and spend a day with Dick McDonald. I want you to come back and write me a report about why you *like* Dick McDonald." I said that was impossible. He said, "I don't care if it's impossible, you're going to do it."

Reluctantly, I called McDonald and, under the guise of coming to Detroit to learn his ideas on what we might do to sell certain national accounts, I arranged to spend a day with him.

Once with him, I discovered McDonald was more like me than not, a guy who had strong family values (like me), who had a genuine love for his associates (like me), and who also had a unique sense of humor. I learned I had not fully appreciated his humor. I learned he is a stand-up guy with lots of character and integrity. It is hard to see integrity when you only see someone from the outside (and even harder when you think you're looking at a jerk). When I began to see how McDonald functioned and how he dealt with his people, I saw someone with great personal influence. I looked at his track record and saw that not only had he been successful personally, he had promoted many people who went on to become successful leaders. Because my boss forced me to look objectively at McDonald and try to remove my bias, I began to see McDonald for what he really was, not what I imagined him to be.

At the end of the day, I liked Dick McDonald, and he hadn't changed one bit. I'd gone to Detroit knowing I had no choice but to find something about him I liked. When I took that perspective, I learned things about him I not only liked, but admired. McDonald was no longer a jerk. After the day we spent together, I felt more comfortable collaborating with Dick on corporate projects, and I was more open to his ideas when we worked together. When I left the company, Dick was one of the few colleagues with whom I maintained a close relationship, and it continues to this day.

This is not to say that, even with the right mind-set, we will find everyone responsive and willing to have a relationship, or even to be civil. While the relationship building that I am describing is effective most of the time with most people, it is not successful with everyone. (Some prospects are so prejudiced about salespeople that they cannot recognize a genuine offer of help even when it's sitting on the other side of the desk.) Nevertheless, the odds for building strong business relationships are on your side, and they can pay off handsomely as Anthony Yim found.

Anthony was working for a company that sold global telecom networks when he received a call from a nonprofit religious organization based in Italy. The caller told him the organization spanned the globe, that it was interested in a telecom network, and that the caller would be in New York in a month. Could they meet?

When they met, the prospect had all the details of what the organization needed. "All of a sudden I woke up," says Anthony. "This could be a very big deal." There was, however, a problem: The people in charge were not interested in so much change; Anthony's contact had to sell it up the line.

"The story he was telling of what he wanted to do was fascinating," says Anthony. "My company fit extremely well with what he wanted to do, so it really made a neat project. But what happened, instead of thinking about the sale and what we were going to sell, I fell in love with the story and the situation. I lost track of the fact that I was making a sale and thought more about working with this guy to try to create something that he could sell internally. As a result, we formed a much different relationship than I usually have with customers." After a productive initial meeting, the contact returned to Italy.

Time passed. Anthony would call the prospect once a month and e-mail him a couple times a month. Anthony decided in this period to educate the prospect about the company, at the time the fourth or fifth largest in the industry. Says Anthony,

"We were not the default company people went with when they couldn't make up their minds. So I used the time to educate him on who we were and what we could do." In addition, Anthony decided not only to differentiate the company, but also to make himself different. He asked himself, "How am I going to do that? Well, continue to be interested in his situation and learn as much as I can about what he wants to do, provide him with extra information, and be available."

As the months began to add up without any apparent movement, Anthony felt pangs of doubt. "When people say they're having trouble getting a project approved, or they're not sure they're going to have the budget, those are big red flags. But I figured a way to keep in touch and put a personal stamp on it. For example, I didn't just send him our white paper on data networking strategy. I would write up a one-page synopsis about what I thought his situation might involve. I hoped he would sense I actually cared and had thought it through, rather than just giving him an attachment on an e-mail to study."

As time went on, Anthony says a couple of interesting things happened. The prospect began to call for advice on what to do next. It was almost as if Anthony's company had become the incumbent supplier. Also, the prospect started to learn more about the company's other products. "He would call and say, 'Do you think this product could work here? I have this other idea.' One thing led to another, and what started out as a two-product sale, became a nine-product deal." Anthony found himself being used as a consultant. He was confident, based on the meaningful dialogue and the relationship, there would be a sale. Because of his relationship, he was able to set up other product demonstrations and have different company people visit the prospect in Italy.

The first phone call was in July, and around Christmas the prospect called Anthony out of the blue. He had approval to go ahead with the project. "Now all of a sudden, I had done the right thing," says Anthony. "I had invested time, whereas other salespeople probably went away and said, 'This guy isn't going to do anything.' I invested the time to build a close relationship, to educate him on my company, and to understand his situation. As we got closer to actually closing the sale, I started pinching myself. No one has this kind of business friendship with somebody who is not your customer. No one sells all the products in the product line at once. No one does. And I haven't done it since."

Anthony's mind-set in establishing and maintaining a relationship with this customer in the end is what made the difference and created a huge sale for his company. Your mind-set—what you think—is the starting point of all great relationships.

KEEP THE FACTS ABOUT HUMAN BEINGS IN MIND

To move up the Pyramid and build strong relationships, you need to ask questions other salespeople seldom ask. You need to think about things other salespeople usually don't think about. Most salespeople seldom consider the 13 fundamental facts about human beings as identified by research:

1. People are not nearly as interested in you, your interests, or your concerns as they are in themselves.

2. Most people want two things out of life: success and happiness.

3. In general, people have a desire to be important.

4. They want to be appreciated.

5. They want you to listen to them with your full attention.

6. People will connect with you only if they feel you sincerely value them.

7. Most people make decisions emotionally and defend them logically.

8. The average person's attention span is very short.

9. People with common interests have natural rapport.

10. People want to be understood.

11. People are drawn to people who are genuinely interested in them.

12. Most people love to teach.

13. People want to associate with others who they believe can help them in some aspect of their lives.

Not every one of these characteristics applies to every human being, and people have them in different intensities. Many will claim that the attributes broadly apply to other people, but not to themselves. Obviously, some people (your mother, your spouse) are interested in you, your thoughts, your concerns. But in general, most people are more interested in themselves than in other people. You distinguish yourself and build a relationship when you demonstrate more interest in the other person than in yourself. Also, people define success and happiness in many different ways. One person may define success as owning a big house and expensive car, another as teaching, a third as working for a nonprofit organization.

Nonetheless, these 13 traits are the place to start. The lesson here is that it ain't about you, it's about them. As Dale Carnegie wrote in *How to Win Friends and Influence People,* "You can make more friends in two months by being interested in other people than you can in two years by trying to get other people interested in you."[1] Because it's about them, you have to understand how they think. I include these 13 facts so you can begin to think as other people think.

Note that you only move up the Relationship Pyramid when you are sincere and genuine. If you do not sincerely value other people, if you are not genuinely curious about them and their lives, you cannot reach the point where they will value a relationship with you. If you are not genuinely interested in other people, they will sense your hypocrisy and neither respect you nor value a relationship with you.

Remember that everybody wears an invisible tattoo that says *Make Me Feel Important.* Psychologists tell us the deepest desire in human nature is the desire to be important. It is our strongest, most compelling, nonbiological hunger. We want to associate with, do business with, and live with people who cause us to value ourselves. Make me feel important and I'll probably like you. I'll listen to you. I'll most likely buy from you.

All you have to do to make me feel important is listen to me. Let me do the talking. Don't talk about yourself, talk about me. Notice me, learn something about me, learn something from me, do something special for me. I want to amount to something. I want to be special and you can help me be that.

ASK THE RIGHT QUESTIONS

As I pointed out in Chapter 6, you need to ask questions to determine whether there is a fit between your product or service and the prospect's needs. You also need to ask questions to determine what someone treasures, which is Step 2 in the relationship-building process. As you learn what someone treasures, you are building the business relationship. I have found that some salespeople, even though they agree with what I've been saying here, do not know what questions to ask.

The goal is to discover common ground—mutual friends, interests, or concerns. If you see no obvious common ground and the other person cares for something about which you know little, learn about it from him or her.

Most of us find ourselves fascinating (even people who claim they are boring) and are flattered when others seem to find us interesting as well. Most of us have stories we like to tell about our experiences—triumphs and setbacks—but few of us have enough opportunity to tell them to an interested listener. If you ask open-ended questions and demonstrate that you are an interested listener—and this cannot be faked—you will build positive business relationships.

But until you know what another person treasures and act on the information in a way that demonstrates you care, the third step in this process, you're at an impasse. People are friendly enough, but you can't get much done. They don't share their real concerns with you. They don't listen to you the way someone who knows and trusts you listens.

By their nature, business relationships are more difficult to initiate than personal relationships. When you meet people in private life, you usually have some common ground. You have a similar interest, a similar political affiliation, a similar religious belief. You live in the same neighborhood, go to the same church, or have been invited to the same party.

When you first meet people professionally, however, you may have no clue whether you share some common ground. You may not know the company values the person represents. You walk into a meeting cold and have to break through all the uncertainty to find the human factor that can bring you together.

So, learning what is important to people is key; learning it from them is crucial. You must get people to talk about themselves. When they share information with you personally, a dynamic starts and accelerates the relationship-building process. This is why the raw information that you might have picked up from a trade magazine, industry gossip, or even a mutual friend about a prospect or customer's favorite vacation or high school experience is less important than hearing the person tell you about it. The act of telling is what makes the difference. When we do icebreaker exercises in our training seminars, I observe people talking about themselves and they are smiling, engaged, and responsive. The dynamic that takes place when two people converse meaningfully is infinitely more important than simply learning someone loves golf or graduated from the Virginia Military Institute (VMI). Use questions like the following to engender those positive emotions:

- What do you do when you are not working?
- Where did you go to school (and how did you choose it)?

- Where did you grow up and what was it like growing up there?

- What was your high school like?

- What do you enjoy reading when you have the time?

- How did you decide to do [whatever the person does] for a living?

- Tell me something about your family.

- Where is your favorite place to vacation?

- What kind of vacation would you like to take that you have not yet taken?

- What community associations, if any, do you have time to be involved with?

- What sports, if any, do you enjoy participating in?

- What sports do you enjoy watching?

- If you could have tickets for any event, what would it be?

- How did you decide to settle in this area?

- What things would you like to do more of, but don't have time for?

- Tell me something about yourself that would surprise me.

These questions are a way to start, and the answer to any one may—should—suggest others to you. Note that these, like all good questions designed to draw out information, are all open-ended. They have no wrong answers. They are intended to get people talking about themselves. Only when people talk about themselves can you uncover areas of common interest and discover what is truly important to them. At this point, you are not asking to understand the customer's business so you can design products and technical solutions to their problems, although that may well become part of the process. Nor is the point to make a new friend, although that may also happen. The point is to build a business relationship and have fun doing it.

Some people you meet in business will be uncomfortable talking about anything personal. But even if they don't want to have a personal discussion—and you can usually pick up on that very quickly by how they respond to a personal question—they will usually want to talk about professional issues. To build a relationship, you must learn what is truly important to the person you are having the conversation with.

You can open doors with good questions and attentive, active listening. "Tell me what you do when you're not working" is much more effective than asking, "Do you have a hobby?" First, many people do not have hobbies. Or they have them, but don't call them hobbies. Second, everybody does something when they're not working. (And if they claim they work all the time, that admission tells you something significant.) What they do when they're not working may tell you something about their feelings for the job. They hate it, and it's only a means to support their nonwork activity. Or they love it and will be running the company one day. It may indicate their family life, their social feelings, or their ambitions.

If you know for a fact the person attended college, you can ask, "Where did you go to college and how did you choose that school?" If you are not sure the person attended college, ask, "Where did you go to school?" People who went to college tend to answer this question with its name. But do not assume

213

someone attended college; especially with someone who may be hypersensitive about not having done so.

You want to be alert not only to coming events, but also to what has just passed. If a customer has just returned from two weeks in Bali, it's an opportunity to talk about the vacation (and incidentally learn something about Bali). How did you decide to go to Bali? What did you like about it? Would you want to go back?

The goal is to listen carefully so you can follow up with a related question. Plan to ask the questions, but don't write them on your cuffs. You should not be thinking, okay, what is my next question? You should be actively listening to what the person is saying. Questions like the ones I suggest here are designed to get another person to open up and begin to talk. Once someone begins to talk, two essentials should take over on your part: a genuine interest in and a natural curiosity about the other person. If you have genuine interest and natural curiosity, follow-up questions will come to you spontaneously.

Remember, even if you know the information, you still need to ask the question and get people to tell you themselves. A dynamic occurs in the interaction when people talk to you about what they like. It makes them like you better and feel differently about you because, by encouraging them to tell you something about themselves, you make them feel better about themselves.

When you ask these questions, you are looking for the activities, goals, and dreams people treasure. If you can encourage people to talk about what they treasure, whether personally or professionally, you begin to build a positive business relationship. But again, don't assume, don't guess, don't presume to know what they treasure. Ask questions that help you understand what is important to them, both personally and professionally. Professionally, you would like to know what the customer and the company are trying to do. Business-related questions include:

- What are some challenges or issues in your work you must deal with that I, or my company, might be able to help you with?
- What is the most frustrating thing about being in your business these days?
- In your opinion, what two or three qualities make a superior sales representative?
- If all work paid the same, and you could go around again, what would you do?

If you know people well, they will tell you almost anything. I sometimes ask people to explain how they get evaluated in their job. If they are evaluated on an issue where you can make a contribution, you can help them improve their performance and benefit yourself. Use the information from your questions to plan further conversations that build a relationship. If I know the company is planning a major expansion, I will suggest suppliers, job candidates, lenders.

To learn what is important to people, you have to ask the right questions. There are hundreds of questions you can ask, and once people begin to tell you what is important, you should think of other questions. Also, once you learn what people treasure, you can plan unselfish and thoughtful acts that demonstrate these individuals are important to you.

WHAT YOU DO

The third element in building a strong business relationship is what you do. Business relationships are not built on mind-set or information—they are built on action. People evaluate our consistent, persistent, predictable actions over time; that's how they conclude who we truly are. That's why everything you do and every interaction you have is so significant. When your persistent, consistent, predictable actions over time say to people that you are a person they need to have a relationship with, then and only then will you reach the tops of their pyramids.

Good relationships exist when people trust you and feel close to you. Your objective in building strong business relationships, therefore, is to encourage customers and prospects to be closer to you and to trust you. To build trust, you must demonstrate your professionalism, integrity, caring, and knowledge (PICK) over time.

Your professionalism is how you do what you do. It is the skill, competence, and character one would expect of people in your profession who are really good at what they do. Your integrity is the quality of possessing and steadfastly adhering to high moral principles, professional standards, or both. You demonstrate your knowledge by what you know well and by sharing your insights.

Your professionalism, integrity, and knowledge tend to be specific to what you do professionally. It is different for a pharmaceutical representative, an engineer, and an accountant. Caring, on the other hand, is not specific to any one profession. Actions that demonstrate you care transcend business, profession, industry, and job description. When you demonstrate that you care, you draw people closer to you, and if you have also demonstrated the professionalism, integrity, and knowledge relevant to your position, you have done all you can do to build that relationship.

You demonstrate your compassion, concern, and thoughtfulness for others by unexpected, inexpensive, and thoughtful acts based on the information people have shared with you. When you have shown over time that you genuinely care about other people—their feelings, desires, dreams—you have shown you are a caring person. Your acts prove you have listened to your customers and they are important to you. They also demonstrate you are not like most other salespeople, which is always a significant goal.

To build the relationship, it is not enough to know what someone treasures to build the relationship. Asking the questions gives you only information. To actually develop the relationship, you must act on the information with gestures and items. I am not talking here about traditional "business gifts"—the golf balls, travel alarm clocks, pen sets, and coffee mugs with the company's logo. Nor am I talking about golf junkets, resort weekends, or dinner and a show.

There are times when, as a generous soul (or as standard business practice in your industry), you may want to provide a relatively expensive gift, but the other person, for reasons of law or company policy, cannot accept one. If you have any doubt, check with human resources (or the company lawyer).

Because the people with whom you want to develop strong business relationships are individuals, I cannot give you a list of surefire actions you can use on them. I can give you some principles and examples, but because each person is unique I have no one-size-fits-all suggestion. Building a strong business relationship requires you to be alert both to what people tell you and to opportunities that demonstrate you listened. Here are some thought starters for ways to show prospects and customers they are important to you.

Be alert to important dates, names, people, goals, places, special concerns, major events, favorite foods, schools attended, and more. Important dates vary by individual, but for most people, their important personal dates—the ones they want remembered—are their birthdays and wedding anniversaries. Other possibilities include the date the company was founded, the date the person joined the company, the date they earned their degrees or graduated from college, and any other meaningful and recurring dates in the person's life.

When you know the date is important, put it on your calendar and do something to recognize it with a phone call, a card, a cake, a pie, or a special meal, which does not have to be expensive. If you know the person would like the birthday generally recognized, make sure the staff knows the date is coming.

Important names include the names of children, spouses, and other people close to the person. For most of us, few things are more important to us than our children. Every time you work with someone, ask about their children and learn their ages. Learn what grades they're in, the activities in which they're involved, the sports they play. Learn their interests, interests they may share with your children, your spouse, even with you. And—key point—*record it somewhere.*

A story about John, my financial planner: I was out one Saturday in mid-December with my four-year-old at a sandwich shop and my cell phone rang. It was John. He asked what I was doing; I told him I was just finishing lunch. He asked if my son had his picture taken with Santa Claus yet; I said no.

John said we should go to a furniture store a good friend of his owned. The friend brings in a Santa Claus one Saturday during the Christmas season and invites good customers to bring in their children to meet Santa and have their picture taken. This is not your ordinary stand-in-line-at-the-mall-and-get-your-picture-taken-with-Santa event. This is Santa sitting in big wing chair, refreshments, and no more than two people in line. The child can sit with Santa for 15 minutes if so inclined. The photographer takes a picture—and it's free.

John said, "This guy looks exactly like Santa Claus. There's nobody here. There's not going to be anybody here. And if you want your son to see Santa Claus and get a great picture, then come down because he's only here until 3:30." I picked up my wife, we went to the store, our four-year-old had a great time, and we came home with a wonderful picture. That's an example of an inexpensive, unexpected, and thoughtful thing. It showed me that John cared, and these are the kinds of things that make it easy for me to want to do business with him.

Personal digital assistants (PDAs) make it easy to record all this information and easy to recall it. When you talk with a customer, ask about Luke and Jennifer and about the niece who is the aspiring fashion model. If you learn that a customer's or colleague's children participate in an activity—football, basketball, soccer, theater, dance, whatever—and if your schedule permits, go watch. Even better, get involved in the activity—

Boy Scouts, Girl Scouts, Junior Achievement, sports. When my daughter was young, I coached girls' softball both for her sake and because one of my biggest customers also coached girls' softball. It was a chance for me to know him away from the office, and we became best friends.

Special concerns include lifestyles, activities, and interests. Lifestyles cover things like vegetarianism, committed involvement in social issues (active volunteer in church or charitable organizations), conscious participation in environmental matters (drive a fuel-efficient car, buy only organic fruits and vegetables). Even a life committed to work could be a lifestyle.

Activities include sports and hobbies: golf, tennis, skiing, bass fishing, hiking, hunting, basketball, Ultimate Frisbee, sailing, woodworking, quilting, gardening, video games, painting, photography, stamp and coin collecting—the list is immense (and publishers produce one or more magazine titles for every one).

Interests include the stock market, international affairs, local politics, religion, books, movies, opera, astrology, football, soccer, baseball—this list is longer than any individual's list of activities because most people have more interests than the activities in which they actually participate.

Once you know someone's special concerns, you can be alert to newspaper and magazine articles related to the interest. As a general principle, pertinent information is almost always unexpected, inexpensive, and thoughtful. Clip and send the review of a new mystery, an article about the benefits of tofu, a story about religious architecture. The Web makes it simple to forward articles and web sites that may be of special concern to a customer. If you share an interest with a customer or prospect, so much the better. If you don't share the interest, use the opportunity to learn about the subject.

Think about the people who might be important to the other person. Important people could be industry figures, well-known executives, or ordinary people who are—or should be—significant to the other person. Whom do you know that this prospect or customer could benefit from knowing? If the person is published, bring copies of the work. If the person is local and accessible, make an opportunity for the three of you to have coffee, a drink, or dinner. Help customers get access to the people they think are important.

What do they want to accomplish in their business and personal life? Find commonalities in your personal goals and the other person's. Suppose you know a woman whose personal goal is to run a marathon. You may not be ready (or able) to run a marathon, but you can be present when she runs hers. Suppose you know someone who wants to create a Japanese garden. You can pick up tips and suggestions. If you know people's personal goals, you can reference them in conversation, be present when they're being achieved, and find some commonality between yours and theirs.

Major events in people's lives may include national or religious holidays such as Thanksgiving, New Year's Day, Christmas, and Yom Kippur, but they also include events such as marriage, promotion, or a death in the family. This last is especially important because people tend to turn away when something bad happens. They act as if an illness, accident, or a business reversal were catching. But usually a thoughtful act at a stressful time can have an incalculable impact.

Find ways to commemorate special events, whether with a note—handwritten or electronic, a fax, a card, or a phone call. Drop a note to say, "Thinking of you." We should always be aware that customers and colleagues may be very different from us, with different holidays, traditions, and histories.

It is often easier for me to develop a business relationship with someone who is dramatically different from me than it is with someone who is more like me. I usually say, "Pardon my ignorance." I admit I do not know much about Buddhism or Guy Fawkes Day or living off the grid. But it is okay to be inquisitive. Most people love to share ideas and experiences that are important to them.

What can you do when you know someone enjoys Mexican food . . . or Japanese . . . or Indian? What if someone loves chocolate covered coffee beans, smoked herring, Danish wedding cookies? Refer people to good, new restaurants in the area or restaurants you know in an area they'll be visiting. You might buy a cookbook on the cuisine they like. Share recipes.

The crucial point is to get to know people. And once you learn important things about them, record them somewhere. I write them down, but others use PDAs, computers, and so on. It really does not matter what you use; the key point is none of us has a good-enough memory that we can do this well without capturing the information somewhere. If you have a customer or colleague for whom college was a peak experience, what can you do with that information? (Nothing if you don't recall it or have some system for recalling it.) At one time, I lived in Charlottesville, the home of the University of Virginia. One of my customers, Charlie Miller, was a fanatic University of Virginia alumnus and lived in Elkton, Virginia, about 60 miles away. One year, the University of Virginia won the National Invitation Tournament basketball championship, and the local paper did a special section on the team and the competition. I remember going to the trash to throw away the section and thinking, "I'll bet one of my customers would like to have this . . . but who . . . ?" Asking the question gave the answer, Charlie Miller.

I wrote a quick note—"Dr. Miller, thought you'd like to see this"—stuck it to the section, and sent the package to him. Two weeks later on my next trip to Elkton, Charlie greeted me as if I were a favorite relative and ordered as if I were his only supplier. We'd had a good relationship before—that's how I knew he was a University of Virginia enthusiast—but that Sunday supplement kicked the relationship up another level or so.

If you are part of a national sales organization, and if you have a customer who still talks about his days at Notre Dame and Notre Dame football or the University of Texas or Ohio State, it is pretty easy to call the representative who covers South Bend, Indiana; Austin, Texas; or Columbus, Ohio; and say, "Send me Sunday's paper," which has a report of Saturday's game. It will cost you about two bucks for the paper and if you're living in Boise, Idaho, you're probably not getting the Sunday South Bend paper.

You can give school paraphernalia. If you know people in the community who graduated from the school, you can connect them over lunch or at a special event. Use them as a resource for children of customers or colleagues who are considering the school. "Colin is thinking of the University of Virginia? He should talk to Charlie Miller. If you'd like, I'll try to set something up."

Some people love to vacation at the same place every year; others want something different every year. Some people are nostalgic about the towns in which they grew up; others are thinking ahead to retirement. Knowing that a place is important and why it's important to a customer or prospect, what can you do about it? Clip and send news articles about the country or the city. Spend time on the Internet and forward information about sights, restaurants, activities. If you know a country, a district, or a city and can recommend a spot, a town, or activity that you know someone would like, do it.

Doing something unexpected, inexpensive, and thoughtful doesn't always produce immediate results—indeed, it may not produce any results at all—but it is still the right thing to do. Not every seed you plant is going to sprout, but if you want vegetables, the more seeds you plant, the better the odds you'll be eating succotash one day.

RELATIONSHIP MAPPING AND PYRAMID HOPPING

Relationship mapping is creating a list of people with whom you must build or initiate relationships. You ought to consciously, deliberately, and strategically map your relationships with four groups of people:

1. *People within the organization who are important to your success:* You need these people to get your job done. They may include customer service reps, warehouse clerks, finance people—everyone who can make your work easier or impossible. They should be a diverse group, not simply your peers in sales or accounting or engineering, but from many parts of the organization.

224

In many situations, we have to try to build these relationships from afar. You may live in Portland, Oregon, but your headquarters is in Detroit. How do you ensure that the people you are mapping are the right people? Then how do you go about building relationships with them from the edge of the country? Most people use e-mail, telephone, and voice mail, but those are not always the most effective way to communicate. The most effective messages are communicated simultaneously by the words you speak and your expression and body language as you say them. This is why a live speaker is more effective than a television image, and a television image is more effective than a voice on the radio. Whenever you use e-mail or voice mail, you reduce the likelihood that you are going to communicate effectively because the recipient cannot see you, your expression, or your eyes.

Perhaps the best way to build long-distance relationships is to make use of the times when you are together at sales meetings, conventions, trade shows, and the like. Before any gathering, make a list of the people you want to know better and create a plan for moving those relationships forward while you are together. Make a point to spend time at breakfast, lunch, or dinner with those key associates. Don't just sit with whoever was in line in front of you; that's what almost everyone else does, and you're trying to be unique, remember?

2. *People external to the organization who are important to your job:* Sometimes it is obvious who the prospective customer is, but in a complex sale it may not be immediately

clear. It is therefore important to map the relationships of everyone involved.

3. *People who are important to the success of your career:* These individuals may be your boss, the human resource director, a mentor, or other people within the company. You need to meet and develop a relationship with these people if they can help you either to understand something about a future opportunity or help you have an opportunity. These resources may also be outside the company— coaches, friends, or a spouse. They are people who will share their insights and experiences, tell you when they believe you are making a mistake, or suggest options you might otherwise never consider.

4. *The people with whom you need to repair a relationship:* For most salespeople, these are prospects or former customers that someone in the organization has alienated. Few of us deliberately offend a customer. But, many of us discover that we have inadvertently caused somebody to become upset with us and we have to try to figure out how to deal with that. A key to sales success is recognizing offense and finding a way to repair the relationship so you can continue to do business with the individual. The offense may not be on a personal level. The customer may be offended because your product didn't perform to specification or the competitive situation forced you to behave in a certain way or your competitors put you in a bad light. Perhaps someone else in your company at some point in the past promised something and didn't deliver.

Interestingly, when I coach people and ask, "Whom do you need to have a relationship with in your company to be more successful," they don't know beyond the obvious: their boss, their boss's boss. But they've never thought through all the implications. They don't know that the HR person makes key decisions. That if they want to ultimately move into marketing, they should develop a relationship with a product manager.

You need to regularly create advocates for yourself, and the only way to do that is to have a comprehensive relationship map. Also, whenever you do relationship mapping and you work for a company, you should always share your map with your supervisor. Your supervisor and you need to agree about who is on your map. A supportive supervisor is unlikely to take people off your map, but probably will add a person or two you never thought of, and may even help you build those relationships.

Relationship mapping and pyramid hopping are two concepts that can change your life. They move you from treating relationships reactively to treating them proactively. You can only be proactive when you master the concepts of pyramid hopping and relationship mapping.

Pyramid hopping is actively pursuing contacts by leveraging the relationships you have with people on your Relationship Pyramid. It is networking on steroids—making a good connection, not just a connection. The strength of the connection is based on where you are on someone's pyramid. By pyramid hopping, you can be more productive and effective because you can access people who are helpful. It is proactively doing something most of us do unconsciously all the time, asking for help from someone we know.

But to do this, we have to know who is on the other person's pyramid. When a friend asks if you know a good plumber and you recommend a trusted plumber, you've helped the plumber hop from your pyramid to your friend's. When someone recommends you as a possible resource and you follow up, you hop from one pyramid to another. Most of us do it to some degree, but we could probably develop the skills to do it much better.

Pyramid hopping is not networking in the ordinary sense. Networking is handing out as many business cards as possible at a business mixer. Networking is what people do when they put their personal profiles on web sites like Friendster, MySpace, Facebook, or register at LinkedIn. A job search web site called SimplyHired is edging toward the kind of pyramid hopping I'm talking about here. SimplyHired has a deal with LinkedIn, so that its users can press a button marked "Who Do I Know?" placed on each job listing. When you click on it, LinkedIn searches its user network to tell you who you know at the hiring company, or who they know who knows someone at the hiring company (assuming you're registered with LinkedIn). This is a kind of technological approach to pyramid hopping that is probably better than nothing, but what I am suggesting is much more personal.

People e-mail me their resumes with a note asking if I can help them find jobs. They expect me to e-mail the resume to somebody else. But this is not pyramid hopping. The actual "hop" or *move* between pyramids occurs when you take the process further to accessing that relationship. So, if someone knows me well enough to send me her resume, she could call me to say, "I'm in the process of looking for a job. Here's what happened. . . . Whom do you know that I might contact in the pharmaceutical business who would be looking for somebody in Texas?" I would tell her the likely people I know and she could legitimately ask, "How would you suggest I go about contacting them? Or would it be better if you contacted them on my behalf if you're comfortable doing that?"

I am glad to call rather than send an e-mail. If someone asks me to forward a resume, I will gladly forward the resume, but the chances of making a connection that way are not very good. If you ask me specifically to help you hop from my pyramid— and you are *on* my pyramid—to another's, I will help you do that. I will always recommend people at the top of my Relationship Pyramid if I'm asked. If a sales manager knows that I have contacts, she may ask if I could recommend a salesperson, and I will recommend someone (or two or three people) at or near the top of my pyramid.

And, depending on the situation, someone does not have to be at the top of the pyramid. I will recommend a reliable mechanic or an accurate accountant who may not value a relationship with me. Even if you are not at the top of someone's pyramid, that person is usually willing to introduce you to other people as long as they believe they run no risk of looking stupid or malicious. That's a hurdle you must clear. Who recommends an inept mechanic or a backstabbing salesperson? You may not be at the top of my pyramid, but as long as I'm sure you won't embarrass me, I'll recommend you.

The challenge is to know who is at the top of someone's pyramid, so you must ask questions. Whom do you know? Whom have you met in the last six months that I ought to know? For example, I recently talked to a good client and asked if he knows someone who runs a large advertising agency. He gave me a name, and I asked if he would introduce me. He said, "Absolutely." The next day he sent an e-mail to the agency chief copying me, saying that we need to meet. I followed up with e-mail; he sent me an e-mail, and we set up a phone appointment.

I could never have hopped from my client's pyramid to the agency chief's without asking him if he knew someone who runs a large ad agency. Conversely, my client would never have volunteered the information because he had no idea I was looking for someone. This is the way pyramid hopping is supposed to work.

TAKE TIME TO ACT

Actions over time do demonstrate your sincerity and substance; they will set you apart from other salespeople. But you have to do them over time. You can't expect to do one thing one time and then get a quid pro quo—and you're not keeping score anyway. Doing unexpected, inexpensive, and thoughtful acts over time demonstrates this is how you operate. This is who you are. Unexpected, inexpensive, and thoughtful acts say, "I thought about you . . . you matter to me . . . and I am different from almost every other person in your business life."

Positive business relationships are built on actions. Unexpected, inexpensive, and thoughtful actions make a statement of who you are and how you treat other people. That doesn't mean an act can never be expensive, but inexpensive is probably better.

I have a friend who is a newspaper publisher. She was getting very frustrated with some of her salespeople because advertising sales were not coming as quickly as anticipated. One of the reps was working with a store in Arizona to establish them as a customer. She would stop by every so often and drop off papers and speak with whoever was in the store at the time, but had been unsuccessful reaching the owner. Yet, the publisher expected that "they should be in our paper; we've been there a lot. They should be buying."

During this process, the paper's editor attended one of our workshops. Once she understood how important it is to establish relationships, she realized this store owner was not going to buy until the paper earned the right to be an advertising medium. The big aha! was the paper had no reason to be upset because it had not yet earned the right to ask for the store's business. It had no relationship. The editor took this insight back to the rep and helped rework the sales plan. Once the sales rep made a focused effort to reach the owner and, on reaching him, began to build a relationship, the outlook for selling advertising space improved considerably.

Abraham Lincoln once said, "If you would win a man to your cause, first convince him that you are his sincere friend." Far too often, we are so concerned about our own agenda that we're not concerned about the prospect's or customer's agenda.

As I have emphasized throughout this book, the winning combination of the right mind-set, an effective sales process, and valuable business relationships will lead to sales greatness. But there's a final piece to this puzzle I must discuss because great sales skills without opportunities are the sure path to the death of a salesman.

CHAPTER 10

YOUR BUSINESS DEVELOPMENT DRIVES YOUR FUTURE

You may have the sales skills of a Zig Ziglar, Jeffrey Gitomer, and Brian Tracy all put together, but if you don't have enough opportunities to ply your trade, you're in trouble. That's why business development drives your future. This is true of commissioned salespeople, salaried salespeople, and entrepreneurs who own their own businesses.

Business development incorporates four activities:

1. Maintain the customer base you have.
2. Grow your opportunities within that customer base.
3. Leverage your current customers for future business.
4. Create new customers.

If you neglect any one of these four elements—maintaining the customer base, say, without creating new customers—your business life will ultimately suffer.

Successful business development requires salespeople to think about many things but two things are critically important: how you spend your time, and how you establish what you want to accomplish.

All salespeople, regardless of their employment situation (and what they think they're doing), are in business for themselves. Either they make something happen at the point of contact with prospects and customers, or they don't.

They can have the right mind-set, be the world's greatest at the DELTA selling process, and build business relationships easily; but if they are not good at developing business and do not create new opportunities for themselves with new clients, existing clients, and friends of existing clients, they are eventually going out of business or quickly will reach a plateau. They are going to be stalled or fired and neither is a happy position to be in. Fortunately, if they have the mind-set, process, and relationships, developing business should not be a major hurdle.

MAINTAIN THE CUSTOMER BASE YOU HAVE

You have to evaluate business development opportunities continuously. To do so, you must analyze your situation seriously and ask: Where is my current business? Where are my opportunities to expand my current business? Where are my customers who are *not* buying from me? Where are opportunities for new business from prospects I don't know or have not met, but need to meet, either by leveraging a current relationship or by cold calling? Finally, perhaps the most important question of all: Where do I need to *stop* spending my time?

There is no business without activity. I have given you a comprehensive approach to thinking like a buyer and using your mind-set, a tested sales process, and a relationship-building process to increase your business. But without applying theses ideas on a routine basis and building a foundation for your business, nothing is going to happen. At the end of the day, it is not just what you know, it is how you apply what you know.

Like lots of people, I think of business development as a funnel. That is not a new concept, but it is salient and relevant. The questions you have to ask yourself are: how many prospects do you have in the funnel? Where are they in the funnel? Your funnel should be filled from several places: customers you are already doing business with, prospects your customers refer (pyramid hopping), and prospects you are reaching out to through direct mail, cold calls, advertising, networking, speaking at events, and the like.

Because the people you already do business with are the ones most likely to continue doing business with you, to give you more business from their company, or to help you get business from somebody else, they are by far the most valuable people in your funnel. There are relatively few of them in the grand scheme of things, because we always have more potential customers than active customers. Ideally, you have cultivated a strong, positive business relationship with these customers. You can have a meaningful dialogue with them at any time, and you have a strong likelihood that you will retain or grow the business you have with them.

LEVERAGE YOUR CURRENT CUSTOMERS FOR FUTURE BUSINESS

The second group of people in your funnel includes prospects to whom you have been referred. Most salespeople know they should actively seek referrals from satisfied customers. Linda Mullen, the Doncaster clothing salesperson, offers a $100 referral fee to her customers, but as every sales manager knows, not every salesperson aggressively follows up their referrals.

Moreover, how you get referred is significant; there are weak referrals and strong referrals (the strongest are pyramid hopping when you are at top of someone's pyramid). A weak referral is someone who says, "You ought to call Bob Rose." You then call Bob and say, "Jerry Acuff told me to call you." It's a referral and a warm call, but it's not very strong. If the person offering the referral makes the call, it will be a stronger referral: "Bob, a friend of mine is going to call and I'd like you to take her call." The strongest referral is when someone not only makes the call, but arranges a meeting for all three of you.

CREATE NEW CUSTOMERS

The third, and largest, group of people in your funnel are prospects you reach through direct mail, advertising, personal contacts, cold calls, networking events, speaking, and the like. I will not say that cold calls never work because I have an acquaintance who has a $15 million business that is based entirely on cold calls, and many other businesses are built on cold calls. But in my experience, that is not the best way to go about building your business—from prospects you do not know. The best way to get business from people you don't know is to make their acquaintance.

Speak at an industry conference whenever you can. Attend a networking event. Join the chamber of commerce. Become involved in something where you are likely to meet people who either can do business with you or who can introduce you to people who can do business with you. You have to put yourself in positions where you can meet people. I am asked to speak at conferences and colleges from time to time. When I speak at universities, I not only have a chance to teach the students, I reach companies that have a relationship with the university and are potential clients. Speaking at conferences is a great way to obtain exposure and develop prospects.

I spoke at a conference in Philadelphia not long ago. I was approached after my 30-minute talk by a group of people who had been sent to the conference to find a vendor that could help them change their sales culture. From the conference, I acquired a client with a very large project for us.

If you can create opportunities to bring customers together to sample your idea, product, service, or offering, that's also a very good idea. We offered a seminar recently that attracted 32 participants from 11 different companies, and 3 of them have already given us contracts. That has more than paid for the cost of the conference.

Put yourself in positions where you can begin to develop relationships that you can leverage. There are many opportunities to do that; however, focus on building a relationship, not on developing the business. The business will come after you have achieved the relationship.

This means your mind-set is central in building new business from people you don't currently know. If you focus on trying to obtain a new customer, you approach the person one way. If you merely try to know the person and then at some point see if it makes sense for you to get together to talk business, you approach another way.

I was at an Arizona Cardinals football game wearing my VMI (Virginia Military Institute) sweatshirt. The guy who was sitting behind me, also a season ticket-holder, tapped me on the shoulder and asked if I was from Virginia. I told him I was actually from Memphis, but I went to school in Virginia. He said he did as well, attending Virginia Tech. Historically, the Virginia Military Institute and Virginia Tech were rivals, so we chatted about the schools and their football programs.

At the next Cardinals game, there was John and we chatted again. Toward the end of the season, I asked him what he did for a living. He said he was in the financial planning business and added that we ought to get together for lunch sometime. As it happened, I didn't care for my financial planner at the time and I enjoyed talking to John. So I agreed to have lunch.

We met for lunch and never did talk about financial planning. We talked about football, we talked about Virginia. We established that I had coached against his brother when his brother was playing in high school, so we had these natural connections. Then he started to ask me questions about my business. He was developing interest, engaging me, learning my situation.

We began to meet for lunch every few weeks. From my time with John, I saw that he was the kind of person I would like to do business with because he had PICK—professionalism, integrity, caring, and knowledge. Eventually he asked whether I had a financial planner. I said I did. He asked if I was happy with him. I said not really. I now know John well enough that had I said I was happy with the planner, he would not have tried to pursue me; he would have known there was not good fit between my situation and his service. But he is now our financial planner managing our financial assets and I have gladly led him to three or four other customers.

This is an example of having a business development mentality that starts with a relationship-building mentality. Start with the relationships you have with your current customers and prospects. What people have you developed relationships with who might give you a reference to someone they know? And how do you put yourself in the position to meet people who might want to do business with you?

The objective is to balance doing your business and managing your customers with creating new business opportunities. If you focus too much on creating business now without thinking about new business for the future, then you are not going to be successful in the long run. So, just as we teach relationship mapping, I practice the concept of new business targeting. Who should I be pursuing as a business target?

SOME PROSPECTS WILL NEVER BUY FROM US

It is a sad fact that certain people to whom we give our invaluable time are never going to buy from us. The reason may be as simple as that the prospect's sister is a rep for the competitive company. No matter how great a selling message may be, a blood relationship usually trumps reason and logic. The prospect is going to do business with the sister's company. Of course, you may never know this reality if you don't ask the right questions, if you don't try to understand the true situation. It is important to use your time to understand the reality.

In addition, there are people who are never going to do business with us because we just never connect with them. While people may say persistence is irresistible, and it may be true in the long run, it is also true that in the long run we are all dead. As Kenny Rogers advises, you have to know when to fold them . . . and when to spend your time on somebody else. Unless you spend time with people with whom you actually have a chance to succeed, you are building a foundation for failure.

As I talked about earlier, prospects who don't buy from you usually don't buy for one of three reasons: Your message doesn't resonate, they have a relationship with somebody else that is difficult to unwind, or they are mad at somebody—often someone in your company (and sometimes you). The only way to do business with them is to learn and try to address the issue.

The ability to assess whether there is a genuine opportunity is vital. In addition, it is also vital to assess not only the prospect's need but also the desire to deal with the problem in a timely basis. Time management is not simply about managing how much time you spend on business development. It is about how much time you spend selling and servicing current customers, how much time you spend pursuing valid prospects, and how much time you spend chasing rainbows. Many people will try to string you along, and if you allow this, you do it at the expense of something else potentially more rewarding.

Salespeople constantly need to ask themselves, "What is the best use of my time?" How we spend our time drives the whole concept of business development. While most salespeople believe the customer's time is invaluable, in reality the sales rep's time is more valuable than the customer's. If a rep misuses the customer's time, the customer has lost an hour or so. Whenever we lose an hour, it could have been at the expense of the biggest opportunity in our life.

Melvin Boaz, at Smith & Nephew, agrees. "I have worked with sales reps as a sales manager where we have been put off for an appointment. You have an appointment for 3:00 and 3:30 comes and they're still not ready to see you. More than once, I've gone back to a secretary or the individual and said, 'I know it's a bad time for you, and it's become a bad time for me, I have other appointments and I need to move on. We will reschedule.'"

As Melvin points out, you could be talking to somebody else who really wants to buy. "The last thing you want to do is just sit in the office waiting. It looks as if you don't have anything else to do, and your time then becomes less valuable in the customer's eyes."

Salespeople who misuse their time by being unprepared, by talking to inappropriate prospects (prospects who can't buy or are professional stallers), or by not following through on customer requests, are on the way to going out of business. If you spend your time with the wrong person, you have lost an opportunity to spend it with the right person.

KNOW WHAT YOU WANT TO ACCOMPLISH

This all starts with having a specific goal about what you want to accomplish because as Napoleon Hill observes in his book *Think and Grow Rich,*[1] anything the mind of man can conceive and believe, it can achieve. Dr. Maxwell Maltz in his book *Psycho-Cybernetics*[2] (which I have read 38 times) said we all have a goal-seeking mechanism, which is like a heat-seeking missile. Nothing is more important than having incredible clarity about what we want to accomplish. Once we have great clarity about a goal, the universe will find a way to bring it to us, to make it happen.

It is not enough to have a plan. You first need goals and you need to write them down. Once you have a goal, develop a plan. Here's how I do it; I always carry a list with me that records my goals, and I review it periodically. My first goal is to reach a certain level of business. The next goal is *Pursue New*

Business at X Company and I have listed the opportunities. Then *Finalize Business* at another current client; not only do I have the business, I have in mind the size of the eventual contract. Then *Finalize New Business* with a list of the people I am currently in dialogue with. The last is *Develop a Target List* to pursue for new business next year and I already have three companies on that list.

The point is to manage your time so you don't spend all of your days selling and servicing current customers, and have no time on business development. If you do, you will have great results this year, and next year you will be wondering what to do with yourself. You have to manage both activities concurrently.

That means you must have some ideas about where you are going to obtain your business or how you are going to leverage your current relationships. It means that, above all, you must have great clarity about what you are trying to accomplish and develop an actionable business development strategy that will drive sales exactly where you want to take them. That in turn means you thoroughly understand your business, your markets, your industry, and your competition.

You must understand your own business. Your manager should not tell you when and where you're losing customers. (By that time, you may be on your way out.) You should know when, where, and why, and have a realistic plan to deal with the losses.

To say the least, a comprehensive knowledge of your business and your industry can be helpful in your business. Know where the people are who make a difference to your success, and where they're going. Identify the up-and-comers in the business so you can develop relationships with them. Be aware of potential mergers and acquisitions within the industry, because if a merger takes place and you don't have a foot in both companies, the odds are 50/50 that you are now toast.

One acronym to keep in mind is ABL—Always Be Looking. You never know where your business opportunities are going to come from, and that means you should craft a powerful elevator speech about what you do. Always be prepared to give it in 15 seconds when someone asks you what you do. I highly recommend the e-book, *Opening Doors with a Brilliant Elevator Speech* by Jeffrey Mayer,[3] which will teach you how to craft a compelling elevator speech. You want to be able to tell someone quickly and compellingly what you do for a living. You never know where you'll find the next opportunity—at a new cocktail party acquaintance, with a seatmate on a plane, or even in an elevator. Business development is a process, not a goal.

You need to be nice to everybody because you really don't know who may help you some day. Have your elevator speech ready because you never know when an occasion will become an opportunity. John certainly did not come to the football game expecting or hoping to find a customer.

If you aim at nothing, you're bound to hit it. But if you know with great clarity what you want and work diligently to get it—and use your time effectively to develop current customers and cultivate new ones—the odds are you will.

Based on my experience as a salesperson, as a sales manager, and as a sales trainer, I am convinced sales greatness requires three elements: the right mind-set, a sales process you execute well, and the ability to build valuable business relationships. At the same time, you must focus on business development.

What's different about the approach I've described is not in business development, because there many books on business development. It's not in the sales process, because there are other sales processes. What has been different here is my emphasis on the right mind-set and on how to build relationships. Without those two elements, there's no way you'll reach greatness in sales.

When you meet with a prospective customer, develop the mind-set that you are attempting to discover whether there is a fit between what the customer wants and what you and your organization can offer. Increase your knowledge of your company, industry, customers, and competitors; practice your messaging to discover the words and phrases that are most engaging; extend your business relationship. Practice the DELTA sales process so customers will hear you out and you can learn their situation and, through emotion and logic, present a solution. Finally, build your business relationships consciously, systematically, routinely, and proactively.

Don't just sell, help customers buy. Don't act like a seller; think like a buyer. Do it, and I am confident you will be dramatically more effective in your sales career and—perhaps even more important—have a lot more fun.

NOTES

Chapter 1

1. Jeffrey Gitomer, *The Little Red Book of Selling* (Austin, TX: Bard Press, 2004).

2. Roger Fisher, William L. Ury, Bruce Patton, *Getting to Yes: Negotiating Agreement Without Giving In* (New York: Penguin Books, 1993).

3. William L. Ury, *Getting Past No: Negotiating Your Way from Confrontation to Cooperation* (New York: Bantam Books, 1993).

Chapter 2

1. Brian Tracy, "You Are the Message," *Selling Power,* July/August 2006, p. 18.

2. Cliff Edwards, "Death of a Pushy Salesman," *BusinessWeek,* July 3, 2006, p. 108.

3. George Bernard Shaw, *Mrs. Warren's Profession,* Act 2.

4. Gerrard Macintosh, "Personality and Relational Time Perspective in Selling," *Journal of Selling and Major Account Management,* Spring 2006, p. 29.

Chapter 4

1. Nicole Gull, "Getting to No," *Inc.,* October 2003, http://www.inc.com/magazine/20031001/sales.html.

Chapter 5

1. Harry Mills, *Artful Persuasion* (New York: AMACOM Books, 2000), p. 133.

Chapter 6

1. Philip Kotler and Kevin Lane Keller, *Marketing Management* (Upper Saddle River, NJ: Prentice Hall, 2006), p. 24.

Chapter 7

1. Dave Lakhani, *Persuasion: The Art of Getting What You Want* (Hoboken, NJ: John Wiley & Sons, 2005), p. 51. Material excerpted from *Persuasion: The Art of Getting What You Want,* is reprinted with permission of John Wiley & Sons, Inc.

Chapter 9

1. Dale Carnegie, *How to Win Friends and Influence People* (New York: Pocket Books, 1982), p. 54.

Chapter 10

1. Napoleon Hill, *Think and Grow Rich! The Original Version, Restored and Revised* (San Diego, CA: Aventine Press, 2004).

2. Maxwell Maltz, *Psycho-Cybernetics: A New Way to Get More Living Out of Life* (New York: Pocket Books, 1989).

3. www.succeedinginbusiness.com.

Index